A MANUAL ON INVESTIGATING CHILD CUSTODY REPORTS

ABOUT THE AUTHOR

Mary E. Lindley:
Selected for inclusion in *Who's Who Among Human Service Professionals* for the 1988 Edition

Member of National Association of Social Workers.

Currently employed as a Child Welfare Specialist for the Illinois Department of Children and Family Services (current specialization is conducting court-ordered custody investigations for courts in seven counties).

FOREWORDS BY:

Dianne Skafte, Ph.D., custody evaluator, author of a book and articles on child custody, considered to be an expert in the child custody area, and currently a consultant in Boulder, Colorado.

Director **Gordon Johnson** (Director of Illinois Department of Children and Family Services) and **Thomas Villiger** (Deputy Director of Division of Child Protection and Division of Program Operations for Department of Children and Family Services in Springfield, Illinois).

Gordon Plumb, Ph.D., Psychologist in Carbondale, Illinois, who conducts numerous custody evaluations for courts and has a high success rate in being instrumental in cases being resolved out of court; Dr. Plumb is also co-author of a book on child custody.

A MANUAL ON INVESTIGATING CHILD CUSTODY REPORTS

By

MARY E. LINDLEY, M.S.W., C.S.W.

Child Welfare Specialist
Illinois Department of Children and Family Services

NASW Register
Diplomate of Clinical Social Work

CHARLES C THOMAS • PUBLISHER
Springfield • Illinois • U.S.A.

Published and Distributed Throughout the World by

CHARLES C THOMAS • PUBLISHER
2600 South First Street
Springfield, Illinois 62717

With THOMAS BOOKS *careful attention is given to all details of manufacturing
and design. It is the Publisher's desire to present books that are satisfactory as to their
physical qualities and artistic possibilities and appropriate for their particular use.*
THOMAS BOOKS *will be true to those laws of quality that assure a good name
and good will.*

Printed in the United States of America
SC-R-3

Library of Congress Cataloging-in-Publication Data

Lindley, Mary E.
    A manual on investigating child custody reports.

    Includes index.
    1. Custody of children — United States.   2. Social
work with children — Law and legislation — United States.
I. Title.
KF547.L56   1988   346.7301'7   88-4896
ISBN 0-398-05487-8   347.30617

DEDICATION

This manual is dedicated to all persons who realize the value, potential opportunities, and challenges that are part of the contested custody area. If just a small percentage of social workers or other mental health professionals take the time to read this custody manual and become motivated to consider the contested custody area as one that is valuable enough to warrant specialization, then this author's efforts will be worthwhile. If other professionals realize that social work has a valuable part to play in the custody area, then the end result may be a significant increase in court orders involving our agency in custody cases at the initiation of judges, attorneys, and persons involved in contested custody litigation.

If it were not for attorneys filing motions for involving our agency in custody cases and/or if it were not for judges ordering our agency's involvement, this author would not have been offered the opportunity to specialize in the custody area. Therefore, I would especially like to dedicate this book to the following judges and attorneys who each in his or her own way made a significant positive contribution to this author's knowledge of the custody area: (1) Judge Leo Desmond, (2) Judge Arlie O. Boswell, Jr., (3) Judge Michael J. Henshaw; (4) Judge C. David Nelson; (5) Judge Terry Foster; (6) Judge Don A. Foster; (7) Judge Donald Lowery; (8) Judge Henry Lewis; (9) Judge John Lundmark; (10) Attorney Robert H. Rath; (11) Attorney Patricia E. Rochford; (12) Attorney Norma Miner; (13) Attorney Bruce D. Stewart; (14) Attorney Michael V. Oshel; (15) Attorney Gary Finch; (16) Attorney Richard Kline and (17) Attorney Rick Hobler.

Two mental health professionals each made significant contributions to this author's knowledge of the custody area. Dr. Gordon Plumb, Psychologist, is involved in completing numerous custody evaluations, is currently co-author of a custody book with this author, and he has contributed significantly to this author's knowledge in the custody areas as well as formulation of major concepts such as major criteria to utilize in the assessment phase of a custody case. Dr. Dianne Skafte (Custody Evaluator, author of a book on completing custody evaluations as well as being author of articles in the custody area, and a person with expertise in this area) has significantly contributed to this author's formulation of the conceptual frame of reference from which investigations are completed. This author has often mentioned Dianne Skafte and some of her ideas in some of this author's reports.

This book is dedicated to all the above persons mentioned, in addition to my family and all litigants and all children who have helped to contribute to this author's appreciation for and understanding of some of the complexities involved in custody litigation.

This manual is also dedicated to Illinois legislators who are responsible for the current Illinois Marriage and Dissolution of Marriage Act which provides the legal mandate for our agency to assume responsibility for conducting court-ordered custody investigations. Children in contested custody cases are fortunate to have concerned legislators who ensure that essential legal mandates will be part of the current legal system and that as the need arises, the legal mandates will be revised. The article entitled, "Does Anyone Care" in Part III of this manual, is especially dedicated to the legislators, not only in Illinois, but throughout the world who are in a position to oppose changes in existing laws or to be actively involved in trying to implement new laws or revise existing ones that will be reflective of serving the best interests of children.

FOREWORD

Only a few decades ago, child custody evaluation was such a rare specialty that no one had yet christened it with a name. Judges would sometimes ask a social worker or psychologist to look into a case and function as a neutral "friend of the court." Sadly, these investigations often consisted of an interview or two and perhaps a quick visit to the mother's house to check for cleanliness. Full fledged evaluations as we know them today—with their structured data gathering, extensive interviews with all significant parties, and careful attention to the best interests of the child—still belonged to the future.

Child custody has become one of the fastest growing fields in the mental health area. Because it incorporates familiar skills such as family assessment and working with children, professionals often assume that expanding into custody work will be an easy transition. They are mistaken. Countless psychotherapists and social workers can share grim tales of their first experiences with custody cases. Entangled by a web of contradictory impressions, manipulated by hard-line attorneys, and embarrassed on the witness stand, many vow never to touch custody disputes again. As they discover, it requires specialized training to formulate good residential and time sharing plans, and to communicate effectively with the court.

Where does one acquire such training? Outside of a few sporatic workshops across the country, little is available. Only those few individuals who join an established evaluation staff will receive the tutoring they need. In fact, until fairly recently, scarcely an article could be found on the subject, let alone a training guide. Consequently, vast numbers of custody and visitation cases are foisted on practitioners who have to mobilize their skills and "wing it" the best they can. One usually ends up wasting many hours groping blindly through a case, often asking the wrong questions and focusing on the wrong issues. Here is where a manual such as Mary Lindley's becomes invaluable. It outlines in clear, specific terms the steps of a good custody evaluation. Questionnaries, form letters, and numerous interview aids are generously provided. Sample custody reports offer many ideas for shaping data into convincing recommendations. Deeper issues of custody work, such as defining criteria for selecting the most beneficial custodian, are explored in detail. Those of us from the earlier years of custody work cannot help but feel a little envious of evaluators today who enjoy the benefit of training material such as this.

A colleague once commented wryly that "in order to do child custody work, you must be one-third mental health professional and two-thirds masochist." There is undeniable pain in dealing with families in the throes of a custody dispute. They represent a select (and often troubled) group, since about 90 percent of all divorcing parents reach agreements about their children without court intervention. Furthermore, we enter the scene not as counselors or comforters, but as evaluators. Few persons feel pleased to have us digging into their lives, no matter how necessary such action is. Nor are we afforded the pleasure of seeing children and adults finally heal from their wounds and begin a new chapter in living. By the time this development occurs, we have long since moved on to the next emergency.

But custody evaluation work offers deeper rewards. We know that our intense effort to probe a child's best interests will carry beneficial consequences for the future. Sometimes these are obvious, as when a girl begins to thrive after moving to the household where she longed to live, or a father establishes a new, vibrant relationship with his kids. Other times the effects of an evaluation are more subtle, as when a mother sees her own behavior in a new light and decides to seek counseling. Thus, both our personal and professional rewards depend on becoming superb evaluators. No one said that the task would be easy. But Mary Lindley has certainly carried us forward with her helpful contribution.

DIANNE SKAFTE, PH.D.

FOREWORD

Court-ordered custody investigations or evaluations are on the increase. Child custody investigations are conducted by both private and public agencies. It is vital that all social workers who conduct a child custody investigation be aware and understand the complexities in the custody area.

Judges continue to be increasingly more conscientious of the long-range needs of children. Judges want to know as much information about the home situation as they can in order to make the best possible custody decision for the children involved.

Judges and attorneys require a holistic picture of the potential permanent environment for the children. They want information about the physical environment as well as the relationship of the child/children to each of the parents (or stepparents, if appropriate). Such information includes information about each of the parents, their financial and emotional stability, each parent's feelings about themself, their children, their life as it is and their goals and future ambitions.

Judges often want to know how the child/children feel about the situation. When appropriate, they want to know which parent the child/children would like to live with and why.

Social workers doing child custory investigations need to understand that custody decisions are very stressful to all involved parties. The workers must be able to sift through these involved parties' emotions to find the truth.

The goal of a child custody investigation is to gather truthful information to help judges in determining the best placement for the involved children. This book includes a careful and comprehensive summary of steps to completing an in-depth child custody investigation. The book also emphasizes the importance of the time which must be spent and the depth to which one must inquire when completing a child custody investigation. It should be an important resource for new and advanced students, as well as for new and experienced workers who may be involved in child custody investigations.

GORDON JOHNSON
THOMAS VILLIGER

FOREWORD

Nothing evokes the worst in otherwise decent people like custody litigation. People who have committed no crime except their inability to live together are thrown into an arena where each goes after the other's Achille's heel with the relentless dedication of a Samurai warrior. One hope for these people and their conflicted children is the rising incidence of court-ordered and lawyer-initiated custody evaluation and investigations. The field of custody evaluation and investigations is just now gaining momentum and acceptance within the legal system. As with any new specialty, there is a tremendous need for literature and research. Mary Lindley's manual is probably the first and certainly the most thorough and pragmatic publication of the "nuts and bolts" of custody investigation for social workers and other custody investigators.

This field is new and unique. Special knowledge and skills are needed in order to at least dull the Samurai's blade until more humane methods are created to deal with this special problem. Mary's manual is not only amazingly complete in its "how to's," it also provides the insight into the typical snags and pitfalls unique to custody investigation which only a well-seasoned veteran of this field can provide. There is no such entity as a simple, straightforward custody investigation.

As does Mary, I hope that this manual (1) kindles the interest of social workers and other mental health professionals to enter the specialty, (2) provides higher education with a text with which to teach this critical human services need, (3) increases the awareness of DCFS administrators as to the appropriateness of custody investigation as part of its mission, and (4) begins to influence legislators to take a closer look at the inappropriate, inhumane, and self-defeating manner in which custody litigation is handled in most states, including Illinois.

GORDON PLUMB, PH.D.

INTRODUCTION

This manual was written for all professionals who are involved at the present time, or have the potential to be involved, in contested custody litigation in the future in a professional capacity. All social workers or other mental health professionals involved in the child custody area are offered this explanatory text for conducting child custody investigations.

The methods and procedures outlined in this manual are not just this author's own theory or philosophy, but a workable methodology that continues to be utilized on an ongoing basis by the author. This manual (based on research and on the author's first-hand experience in custody specialization) is one that can be utilized by professionals not only in Illinois and other states, but throughout the world. To this author's knowledge, this manual is the only one in the country written by a social worker about conducting child custody investigations.

Another goal in writing this manual is to share ideas with other professionals with the hope that the methods outlined (including the forms) will be beneficial to the professionals currently involved in conducting custody investigations or evaluations, and will provide an insight into the potential for professional involvement and specialization for those other professionals who have not been involved, but would consider becoming involved in the custody area.

Another use for this manual would be for instructors in colleges and universities throughout the country to consider utilizing this manual as one of the books to be read by students majoring in social work, sociology, psychology, law and other related professional areas. Students currently in the above areas may be the potential service providers in the future for litigants, children and courts in contested custody litigation.

Part III of this manual includes a discussion of relevant custody issues. One of the author's goals is that legislators, not only in Illinois but throughout the world, will realize the rights of innocent victims (who are children in the middle of a contested custody proceeding) to be provided with services from professionals who are legally mandated to conduct child custody investigations.

The feasibility of revising the current laws, and implementing some of the suggestions for the future listed in this manual, might prove to be beneficial to children in contested custody cases. Laws need to be initiated, maintained or revised, with the goal of children involved in custody litigation being provided with professional services which will help enable them legally to live in the most nurturing environment possible. Service providers need to be knowledgeable in the complexities of contested custody and need to possess the skill and expertise in providing quality services not only to children, but to the courts.

May this manual be of some benefit to each person who reads it, including social workers, other mental health professionals, judges, attorneys, administrators in state agencies, legislators, students and litigants. If the end result of writing this book results in current or potential benefits to children in the middle of contested custody litigation, then all the time, effort, research, expense and devotion to this works completion will be worthwhile. May this be a professional contribution to an area that deserves ongoing and continued professional involvement (the custody area).

ACKNOWLEDGMENTS

I am very grateful for Dianne Skafte and her book—*Child Custody Evaluations, A Practical Guide*—which has been invaluable to me in helping to confirm many of the ideas and approaches I was already utilizing in completing investigative custody reports for the court. Other suggestions in her book helped me to make some revisions procedurally so the studies can be more informative, more concise, and more beneficial to the court system.

I am especially grateful to the Saline County Circuit Court (particularly Judge Arlie O. Boswell, Jr., and Judge Michael J. Henshaw) for their numerous court orders involving our agency in the completion of investigative custody reports and to my supervisor, Lyndel Stacey, for giving me the opportunity to specialize in this area. Illinois Department of Children and Family Services Director, Gordon Johnson; Deputy Director of Department of Children and Family Services, Thomas Villiger; and Assistant Regional Administrator, John Allen; are three administrators who have been very supportive of my specialization in the custody area, and I will always be grateful for their encouragement, support and willingness to allow the initiation of innovative ideas in areas in which our agency is legally mandated to provide services. Georgia Cooper, Department of Children and Family Services employee in Springfield, Illinois (who previously worked in Interstate Compact), has also offered much encouragement.

Three attorneys helped tremendously in regard to my being motivated to analyze my approach to completing custody reports and to try to use my knowledge and social work skills so that I can do the most effective job possible. These attorneys are Robert H. Rath, Pat Rochford, and Norma Miner. I especially want to express my appreciation to Attorney Robert H. Rath and to his secretary, Joyce Browning, for their help in getting this manual typed, for offering suggestions regarding the content of the material included, and for offering encouragement in this worker's goal of completing this manual.

Department of Children and Family Services worker, Debbie Greer, began that initial spark of interest in my sharing my thoughts, research, and experience with others. I also had an interest in contributing a beneficial service to the custody field.

Thanks go also to Clara, Sandy and Debra for contributing their typing skills in typing volumes of pages in this worker's preparation of final reports to the courts.

My sister, Dr. Marie Childers, inspired me to be involved in a project that would be challenging career-wise and would be creative. My dad (now deceased) and mother (David and Christine Turnipseed) as well as my niece, Lisa, have always been supportive of my interests and goals.

I also want to express my thanks and appreciation to all persons who take the time to read this manual. This author's hope is that the manual will be of benefit to all professionals involved in the custody area, as well as to the litigants and children who are in the middle of contested custody litigation. After all, a professional involved in conducting a custody investigation or evaluation has primary responsibility to the court and to the children in the middle of contested custody litigation.

Last, but not least, I appreciate my husband (Ray) and son (David Aaron) for their patience with me in my spending a considerable amount of time, thought, research, and effort in writing this manual.

Figure 1.

CONTENTS

A MANUAL ON INVESTIGATING CHILD CUSTODY REPORTS

PART I

Chapter 1

THE NEED FOR PROFESSIONAL SPECIALIZATION IN THE CUSTODY AREA

When I began completing the majority of the investigative custody reports for a seven-county area in connection with my employment as a social worker for the Department of Children and Family Services, I discovered the number of orders from the court, for our agency's involvement in completing an investigation and report as specified in the Marriage and Dissolution of Marriage Act pursuant to Sec. 605(a), Chapter 40, Illinois Revised Statutes, had been gradually increasing.

The majority of the contested custody proceedings I have worked with have not involved the typical contested divorce case in which the husband and wife both were legally competing for custody of the child or children and both could provide comparable home environments that would adequately meet a child's physical, emotional, educational, medical and spiritual needs. Instead I found that the cases ranged from a study being ordered involving no contested custody and only one person filing for legal custody to a case involving five separate parties to the custody proceedings—all trying to obtain legal custody of a child.

Cases have been about parents trying to get a change of custody due to a belief that the child or children involved were in an environment in which the child allegedly was being neglected and/or abused. Other cases might concern a relative trying to legally take a child away from a natural parent due to alleged neglect or abuse of the child or due to a disapproval of a parent's current lifestyle. I have found the majority of the cases to be quite complex, fascinating, and very challenging in terms of trying to assess all factors relevant to a custody decision to determine which permanent living arrangement would be best for the child.

In what I consider to be the traditional approach to completing investigative custody reports, many social workers would make a home visit, talk to the adults who were parties to the custody proceeding, would occasionally interview the child (if old enough to give relevant information) and would sometimes talk to collaterals. No conclusion, assessment or recommendation was usually made. Some studies would be completed in a few hours or less. The interview with the adults consisted mostly of obtaining background information such as birth dates, marital history, employment and education.

The interview with the child might be quite brief and was not always done with the idea of what type of information it is important to obtain from this child that would benefit the court.

Collateral interviews (if completed at all) might include such questions as asking for information relevant to the study without any clear focus as to what would be most beneficial. A note that Mr. Jones or Mr. Smith were excellent parents might be included without any further questions from the social worker as to what *first-hand concrete observations* there were which would reinforce this particular conclusion about parenting abilities. Vague information without determining the reasons for a person's opinions or general impressions is a great fallacy.

It is also important to consider the collateral's comments in relation to values or beliefs. For example, if Mrs. Jones talked about how well mannered Mrs. X's children are due to Mrs. X's excellent discipline techniques, it would certainly be viewed in a different light if a worker knew in fact that Mrs. Jones defines "excellent discipline" techniques as consisting of abusive techniques in dealing with children—to the point that a child is injured as a result of the discipline. Mrs. Jones, in fact, might be an abusive person herself and view Mrs. X's discipline techniques from her own value system that could be in conflict with social work values and practices.

In trying to read as many publications and books as possible about family assessment or evaluation in custody cases, this worker only found two books in 1986 that had been published, both of which this worker ordered, read, and has as a reference. To this worker's knowledge, there is no manual or publication written in this area by a social worker or written for social workers to use in completing custody investigations. Besides the book written by Dianne Skafte mentioned in the acknowledgement section of this manual, the other book is *Family Evaluation in Child Custody Litigation* by Richard Gardner. More books were found to be in print on Japanese Art than on child custody. I am not implying that the subject of Japanese Art is not important; I am saying, however, that the subject of child custody is very important. It seems obvious that a much needed area for professional concentration and writing is the area of contested custody..

In the *Department of Children and Family Services Child Welfare Services Practices Handbook* — one section deals with eligibility for child welfare services from the Department of Children and Family Services. The distinction is made as to how the Department *MUST* serve and as to how it *MAY* serve. Included in the categories that *MUST* be served are court-ordered custody investigations and supervision under the provisions of the Marriage and Dissolution of Marriage Act as well as studies requested through the Interstate Compact Office. Since this is an area of service we *MUST* provide by law if ordered by a judge, I have a firm belief that professional social workers have an obligation to use knowledge, skills, experience, and expertise to provide the best quality service possible. Many court orders specify that advice and/or recommendations by the Department of Children and Family Services worker be made as part of the investigation of all relevant factors in determining custody.

Many social workers (as well as myself) have been guilty of sending reports, reflecting a summary of information obtained by having the parties to the custody case fill out a detailed questionnaire. An investigative home study should include making a home visit with detailed observations and which would be strengthened by having a photographer take detailed pictures of each room in a person's house. I am convinced that changes are needed to improve the quality of custody reports. Social workers owe much to the courts, attorneys, and clients involved in custody litigation. Professional court reports should include an assessment of each litigant's current living arrangements, as is now the case.

It has been this worker's experience that many times during the completion of an investigative home study, a social worker may collect a wealth of information and observations but then do nothing further and not offer any type of assessment or recommendations. Social workers can make assessments about the potential risk to a child if returned to the home of an abusive parent or remains in a parent's home where allegations of abuse or neglect have been made. It seems logical to this worker that investigative skills should be utilized in all areas of our work— particularly those which *MUST* be served.

In 21 years of working for the State of Illinois, this worker cannot ever remember attending workshops or training sessions involving the conducting of custody investigations. This manual offers a practical guide for social workers or other mental health professionals in completing custody investigations. Presented are ideas this worker found workable and useful.

The following chapters reflect a broad overview of ideas and experiences in this area.

There is a definite need for this type of manual due to the following: (1) an increase in contested custody cases; (2) the complexities involved in custody cases; (3) the lack of information available in this area; and, (4) the lack of uniformity in terms of procedures utilized in completing custody investigations.

An attorney usually obtains a one-sided picture of a custody dispute (his client's perception of the situation). A judge has to depend on testimony that sometimes does not reflect all the information (particularly negative information) a person may have if he is subpoenaed to testify on behalf of one of the parties to the custody proceeding. A person testifying in behalf of Mrs. Smith may mentally sift out information (either consciously or unconsciously) before answering questions and leave out or not volunteer relevant information that is negative. Testimony is usually contradictory and may not relate at all to the parenting abilities of the litigants.

If psychologists or psychiatrists are ordered by court to complete evaluations, the end result might be beneficial or may consist of no recommendations to help the judge. A psychologist or psychiatrist traditionally might complete an evaluation in his/her office in an hour or less in direct interview with a person. It would be rare to expect a psychologist or psychiatrist to make an actual home visit to a client's home even though *a home visit would be extremely beneficial in the assessment process.* A home visit provides information that cannot be provided by any other method, and helps an investigator get a clearer picture of the type of home environment to be provided.

A person may be determined to be an emotionally healthy person with excellent parenting abilities in a psychological evaluation. This same person may have a history of leaving his/her child repeatedly for long periods of time and might verbalize (outside of an interview situation) resentment of having child care responsibilities. A litigant may want the status of being a "mother" or "father" without having to assume any parental responsibilities.

Psychologists or psychiatrists may not check with any collateral resources and therefore would miss a sometimes valuable source of information about a person's typical behavior outside of an office interview setting. A person may demonstrate (verbally) excellent parenting skills but may be living in an environment reflecting his inability to manage money, pay bills, and provide for a child's minimal needs for adequate food, clothing, shelter and medical care.

East profession has valuable knowledge that can be contributed to the custody field, but it is the social worker who is in the unique position to view all factors contributing to a person's ability to adequately meet the physical, medical, emotional, educational, and spititual needs of a child.

If a social worker has a specific assessment or recommendation at the completion of an investigation, and doesn't convey this recommendation or assessment, this is negligence on the part of the social worker. It would be analagous to a physician who completes a thorough examination of a patient, reaches a diagnosis, but decides to keep his diagnosis a secret, choosing not to tell the patient. The physician's knowledge, skills, and expertise would have been wasted. As social workers, let's not be like the physician in the above example in the way we complete investigative custody reports.

Chapter 2

OBTAINING BACKGROUND INFORMATION

In the Appendix section is this worker's own outline of a form requesting background information that can be mailed to parties in a custody proceeding and the worker can request that it be returned prior to any home visit or interview with the litigant. This saves the worker valuable time, cuts down on secretarial time in typing reports, and can give the worker an idea about each person's perception of the custody issue — before an actual interview. The amount of time and/or completeness that a person takes in completing the form can be an indication of each person's interest in custody. The interview and home visits now can be utilized for asking relevant questions designed to help assess each person's parenting strengths and weaknesses.

The form traditionally sent to persons seeking custody has information such as height, weight, color of eyes, etc. — information that is usually worthless in terms of assessing parental abilities. If a child had a medical problem with being overweight and gaining additional weight would be a risk factor in terms of the child's future health, this would be relevant. But when the worker makes her first in-person interview, one can quickly see that a person is overweight without knowing whether a person weighs 300 pounds or 290 pounds. Furthermore, a person with a weight problem in all probability will not write down accurate weight on a form anyway. The form used previously specified husband/wife and, as mentioned, the form is totally inappropriate in most of the custody cases. The form in the Appendix may be completed by anyone who is a party to a custody proceeding and saves valuable time.

For purposes of this manual, the term "litigant" is used interchangeably with the phrase "person or party to a custody proceeding."

Chapter 3

INTERVIEWING PARTIES TO THE CUSTODY PROCEEDING *** INCLUDING THE IMPORTANCE OF THE HOME VISIT

The following questions are examples of relevant information that can be obtained in interviews with parties to a custody proceeding. The observations during a home visit can help the worker assess the following: (1) a parent or parent substitute's relationship and interaction with a child; (2) techniques utilized in discipline; and (3) determining if a parent or parent substitute's behavior (in terms of parenting abilities) is consistent with the verbalized philosophy of child rearing.

All questions asked and observations made during home visits and interviews should be utilized in assessing each litigant's parenting capacity (strengths and weaknesses). The *quantity of time* each litigant spends in child care responsibilities should be assessed in addition to the *quality of child care* each litigant demonstrates.

Current parental functioning should also be viewed in relation to the litigant's age, experiences, and the potential for positive growth in terms of parenting skills. For example, a grandparent of a child involved in a custody proceeding would be expected, in all probability, to possess more parenting skills and to have a more stable home environment than a 17 year old natural parent of the child. *Remember that the child has a right (in this worker's opinion) to be raised by a natural or adoptive parent unless there is factual evidence to substantiate that this plan is not in the child's best interest.*

In summary, view the present situation of each litigant in relation to the following: (1) potential for future parental functioning; (2) age of the child; and, (3) age of a litigant in relation to all other relevant factors to determine the best long-range plan for the child.

QUESTIONS FOR ADULTS IN CHILD CUSTODY LITIGATION TO HELP EVALUATE EACH PERSON'S PARENTAL CAPACITY

1) Tell me about each child's strengths and weaknesses.
2) What do you like best about each child?
3) What do you like least about each child?
4) Is any child exhibiting any current behavior problem?
5) Is the child the kind who likes to come into your bed in the morning, especially on weekends and holidays?
6) Describe a typical day for you.
7) How much time do you spend alone with each child in recreational or other activities each day? What kinds of activities do you participate in with each child?
8) What things have you found you have to punish children for?
9) What have you found to be the most effective method of discipline for each child?
10) What is the best way to handle a child's temper tantrum?
11) What would you do if you found your child was physically fighting with another child?
12) What would you do if your child began shouting profanities directed at you?
13) What would you do if your child was diagnosed as being mentally retarded?
14) What do you consider to be the most important values to teach a child?
15) How is each child doing in school (if school age).
16) Do you ever talk to school staff in regard to each child's progress in school?
17) Do you have any problems that would interfere with your ability to assume parental responsibilities for a child?

Chapter 4

INTERVIEWING CHILDREN

If children are old enough to gain relevant information from, it is important to interview each child separately, preferably in a neutral setting such as the school. It is important to make the following assessments: (1) assess a child's understanding of why the worker wants to talk to the child; (2) assessment of the child's understanding of what it means to tell the truth; (3) an assessment of whether or not a child has been coached or "brainwashed" by a party to the custody proceeding; and, (4) an assessment of the child's past pattern of whether or not he is known for being very honest or whether he routinely tells stories not verified by any facts.

The worker should stress before the child is asked any questions that the worker is interested in the child's view of areas covered. It is helpful to stress that the child should answer each question by telling the truth and to tell *his own ideas* and not just reflect what he has heard or thinks a worker may want to hear. This worker can remember one particular instance in which a child's answers were identical to the adult's answers and answers consisting of words not usually in the vocabulary of that particular aged child.

In this worker's experience, it is essential to ask open ended questions and to ask the child questions such as "What do you like best about living in your mother's home"? (about each adult's home that is a party to the proceeding). It is also important to assess during the home visit whether or not the child's answers to questions are consistent or inconsistent with a child's behavior. For example, one child repeatedly told this worker that she preferred living in her mother's home and talked about her dislike for her father. In observations of the child with her father, she spontaneously demonstrated much physical affection toward her father and related to him in ways that did not seem consistent with the verbal responses. More data obtained during the investigation revealed that the child was merely verbalizing her mother's ideas regarding what the child's preference should be. Enclosed is a list of questions that can be used in interviews with children. This worker need not elaborate on the

11

waste of time in trying to interview a child that is three or four years old or younger. Our son's explanation for getting a scratch was that he got it while in a tornado is one illustration of this point.

QUESTIONS UTILIZED IN INTERVIEWING CHILDREN IN A CHILD CUSTODY EVALUATION

First assess child's ability or understanding of telling the truth.
 1) What is your name?
 2) How old are you? What kinds of activities do you enjoy?
 3) What grade of school are you in (if school age)?
 4) What is your understanding of why I want to talk to you?
 5) Can you describe your mother, your step-father, if appropriate?
 6) Describe your father for me, your step-mother, if appropriate.
 7) What do you like best about being in your mother's home?
 8) Is there anything about being in your mother's home that makes you unhappy?
 9) What do you like best about being in your father's home?
10) Is there anything about being in your father's home that makes you unhappy?
11) Do you ever get into trouble at your mother's or father's home?
12) If so, what do you get in trouble for in each home? What method of discipline is used by each parent?
13) Describe a typical day at your mother's house?
14) Describe a typical day at your father's house?
15) What kinds of activities do you and your mom do together? What kinds of activities do you and your dad do together? Do you have any idea who spends more time with you, your mom or your dad?
16) If you had three wishes, what would you wish for?
17) Do you have a preference regarding who you would rather live with? If so, what is it and reasons for your preference?
18) If you had a problem you needed to discuss, who would you want to talk to and why?

Chapter 5

INTERVIEWING COLLATERALS

Interviewing collaterals is a valuable source of information, particularly in terms of assessing the extent of truth, if any, to allegations listed in petitions. This worker would especially emphasize the importance of not just interviews with one or two collaterals a person lists as a reference, but also the importance of interviewing collaterals not listed by litigants if the collateral would be a potential source of relevant information (depending on your assessment of what type of additional collateral interviews are needed).

Consider the example of a parent who filed for custody of a child and obtained temporary legal custody of the child. An allegation was made that the child was not actually living in that particular parent's home but in a relative's home (a relative who had no legal involvement and was not a party to the custody proceeding). In-person contacts with neighbors can confirm the probable truth of such an allegation. If several neighbors have never observed a child in the parent's home but had daily contacts with the parent, and a home visit confirms no sleeping arrangements or toys for a child of the age of the one in the custody dispute, then the allegation might be true. An investigative study which might have been made that would not include any contact with collaterals could easily result in an assessment that this particular parent had excellent parenting skills (based on answers in an interview) when in reality this parent did not even want to assume the child care responsibilities for the child. In this particular example, the child would have been too young to verbalize.

Hopefully a worker realizes the importance of getting a total picture of a situation, and not just focusing on one or two tasks in completing the investigative custody report. It is also important to verify employment (if appropriate) and amount of income.

A worker should obtain relevant information from school staff in regard to each school-age child. Information should include: the child's behavior, attitude, academic abilities, and/or achievements, observations

13

of personal hygiene of each child, attendance, and involvement of parent or parent substitute in attending school conferences.

Questions that can be utilized in interviewing collaterals follow:

INTERVIEWS WITH COLLATERALS

1) Do you know both parties or each party involved in the current custody proceedings?
2) How long have you known each person?
3) What is the nature of your relationship or contacts with each person?
4) Have you had an opportunity to observe each person with the child or children involved in the custody litigation?
5) What are your observations?
6) What would you consider each litigant's strengths to be in terms of their parenting abilities?
7) What would you consider each litigant's weaknesses to be in terms of their parenting abilities?
8) Are there any additional direct concrete observations you have that would be beneficial to know in regard to either litigant's parenting abilities?
9) Are you aware of any problems a litigant has that would interfere with their ability to provide a home environment that would meet the physical, emotional, spiritual, medical and/or educational needs of a child?

Additional questions may need to be asked, depending on the allegations in the petition, the information being given by the collateral, and the type of information expected by collaterals who are professionals. Additional questions are usually always needed to clarify the exact nature of a collateral's observations of a litigant's relationship with a child (specifically the approximate date or dates of the collateral's contacts with the litigant and/or the child, amount of time the collateral spent in each observation, and the total number of relevant observations). It is important to know whether or not a collateral is related to one of the litigants as this may affect the perceptions of the collateral. It is essential that any allegation of medical neglect must include an interview or interviews with a physician as part of the investigative procedures.

Chapter 6

WRITING THE FINAL INVESTIGATIVE
CUSTODY REPORT

Persons who are familiar with our previous style of writing final reports will be relieved to find out that we are in the process of changing the final written report to a format that will be more concise but hopefully more beneficial and more informative. Attorneys, judges and secretaries will be particularly pleased with our decision to dictate the final report in a concise manner without losing the important relevant content. Some of our previous reports were detailed enough and lengthy enough to provide information that could be the subject matter of a serial on television! As mentioned in the acknowledgement section, primary credit for this revision is given as the result of reading Dianne Skafte's book. After much thought in terms of the revised procedures, this worker does not really believe that the quality of the report would be compromised.

The final report is an end result of the on-going assessment undertaken during each of the following procedures outlined in chapters one through five. The following assessments are completed prior to the final report: needs of each child; parenting capacity of each adult who is a party to the custody proceeding (including not only past history of parental functioning, but also current parental functioning, and the prognosis for future parental functioning). The final assessment decision results in a recommendation of which home environment will best meet each child's needs (including physical, emotional, spiritual, educational, and medical needs) in terms of a long range plan for the child with the primary focus being on the best interest of each child. The best long range plan should be viewed in terms of the rest of the child's life (at least until age 18 or 21) and not just considering what the best plan would be for this year or this month.

Try to be aware of any prejudice a worker might have—as a worker's own personal feelings should *not* influence a worker's final decision in

15

terms of a recommendation. For example, a mother might live in a $200,000 house, have just won $12 million in the lottery, have a live-in housekeeper, and verbalize more parental strengths than weaknesses. The father may be unemployed, be receiving financial assistance from the Department of Public Aid, may be living in a small mobile home, and demonstrate limited parenting abilities. Assessment of some of the above factors might influence one to lean toward the mother in terms of physical environment, the financial advantages to the child, and the mother's superior parenting ability. If further evaluation reveals the following: the mother's I.Q. is 180, she is a perfectionist who expects that her child will be an "A" student, the mother perceives the child to have no limitations—this would be an important consideration in determining the child's best interests—especially if the child is diagnosed as having a severe learning disability and the prognosis is poor for the child's ever being able to achieve more than a "C" average in special education classes. Even though 9 out of 10 workers would probably quickly determine that the mother's living situation would be a preferable one in meeting a child's needs, however, in considering this particular child's needs in relation to the above factors, it may be in the child's best interest for the father to obtain legal custody, particularly if the following criteria are met by the father: (1) he is able and willing to provide care that would not be considered neglectful or abusive in any way; and, (2) the child has strong emotional attachments to the father. The worker hopes that the above example helps illustrate the *importance of not only following all steps in the assessment process, but the importance of viewing the total picture with an emphasis on the needs of each particular child.*

The final recommendation should be the end result of the worker's (1) gathering relevant detailed information from persons who are a party to the custody proceeding; (2) information obtained from interviews with a child or children (if appropriate); (3) interviews with collaterals; (4) observations from home visits; (4) relevant information from the court file; (6) the assessment of needs of each child; and, (7) assessment of the parental functioning of each litigant. The recommendation should be the end result of many hours of time, effort, thought, interviews, observations, and viewing the relevant factors as a total picture and not just as individualized pieces of information. It is recommended that a minimum of 14 to 17 hours be spent in completing an investigative custody report involving two adults and one child, provided there are no allegations that would require more time. Naturally the greater the number of issues and allegations involved as well as the greater the number of adults and/or children there are in the custody litigation, the more time would be required to complete a thorough report that would reflect quality work resulting from thorough assessment of all relevant factors. In this worker's experience, the custody field is one that has an increasing need for social work skills and one in which a worker at least knows that before a worker receives an order signed by a judge, there is a pending case in court. If a social worker's skills can benefit a judge in his decision—one that will have a profound effect on the rest of the child's life—then it is time, money, and effort well spent and worthwhile. In this worker's opinion, there is a need for specialization in the completion of investigative custody reports by Department of Children and Family Services staff. There is also a need for uniformity of procedures followed by agency workers, not only in Illinois, but throughout the world.

This worker knows of no professional who is always 100% accurate in utilization of knowledge, expertise, and skills but each professional still has a professional responsibility to reflect that his/her skills are used to the maximum extent possible.

It is this worker's experience that a custody decision may mean the difference to a child of whether or not that child may be forced legally to live in a home environment where the potential for abuse or neglect is high or already exists. As should seem obvious to any social worker, there is no law existing (to this worker's knowledge) that an abusive or neglectful parent cannot file for divorce and cannot file for legal custody of children. In actuality, the same family that may be involved in a contested custody case and an investigative home study might also be involved at the same time in a Department of Children and Family Services investigation in which allegations of abuse and/or neglect are pending regarding one or both adults who are parties to a custody proceeding. It is a mistake for a social worker to make any generalizations or assumptions regarding a contested custody case. Hopefully this manual will reflect that a social worker should not try to apply "pat answers" in making a recommendation concerning custody. For example, a mother should *not* automatically be recommended for custody of a baby girl (even if the baby is being breast-fed). Applying "pat answers" would be an injustice to the social work profession.

Chapter 7

TESTIFYING IN COURT

Testifying in court and particularly being cross-examined on the witness stand about the contents of a worker's investigative report is a reality as this worker has testified in several custody hearings in several different counties.

One soon learns the importance of not only writing a report based on a thorough assessment but also on being certain to write down accurate information including: (1) notes as to dates of interviews; (2) approximate time spent in each interview; and, (3) the reasons for the worker's methods of assessment utilized in the completion of the investigative custody report. This worker had this importance well demonstrated in being made to undergo the impact of 3 ½ hours of cross examination during testimony in a custody hearing. It is important when writing the final report to always keep in mind that whatever is included in the report should be included as a result of *sound judgment based on a thorough assessment of all relevant factors in the case.* A worker needs to be prepared to be cross-examined on the witness stand regarding the content of any information included in the report.

If a judge reached a decision that is contradictory to a social worker's recommendation or assessment, a social worker should keep in mind that just as a judge does not have knowledge and skills in the social work field, a social worker does not have knowledge and skills in law. The concept of the best interests of the child is vague enough that what a social worker views as the best interests of a child from a social work perspective may or may not be legally feasible in viewing the best interest of a child from the legal perspective based on evidence presented in court. The judge, just as the social worker, is making his decision based on his experience, skills, and expertise in law and has a duty to make his decision based on his perception of the best interests of the child.

Another fact to consider is that judges, just as social workers or any other professional, possess differing skills and expertise in the custody area.

In this author's opinion, Judge Leo Desmond in White County, Illinois,

18

has more knowledge and understanding of the complexities involved in the custody area and of future implications of court decisions than any judge this author has ever met. If Judge Desmond's decision was contradictory to this author's assessment of a case, this author would in all probability conclude that this author lacked crucial relevant information. This author's respect for the wisdom of some of the judges, such as the Honorable Leo Desmond, would result in a belief that a fair objective court decision was made.

All professions have persons who demonstrate such exceptional knowledge and expertise in their profession that those particular individuals have earned the utmost respect of others. Judges who demonstrate exceptional expertise in the custody area, such as the Honorable Leo Desmond, find that their judgment is highly respected by professionals, and their decisions will always be based on the best plan for each child.

The social worker can feel like she is hopefully a credit to the social work profession if she is doing the following: (1) utilizing her skills, knowledge, and expertise in the social work field to the maximum; and, (2) is motivated and dedicated to demonstrate verbally and behaviorally that she is trying, to the best of her ability, to utilize her social work skills in attempts to play at least a small role in making a beneficial and significant contribution to the specialty of contested child custody.

Utilizing the techniques outlined in this manual would be more beneficial if a court order afforded the opportunity for the same social worker to assess all parties and children in the same contested custody proceeding, which is not always feasible. One possibility would be for the worker closest to the court of jurisdiction in the custody case to assess any party living in another part of the state or out of state when that particular party comes to the area of court jurisdiction prior to the court hearing. The court order could specify that all parties and children in the custody proceeding are to be available to this particular worker and cooperate with the assessment.

A worker can still utilize the methods outlined in this manual in evaluating even one person and/or child; however, unless the other worker or workers involved in the same case used comparable methods in completing investigative custody reports, the total picture presented to the judge would still lack relevant information regarding the person or persons for whom the study was completed in what this social worker would conclude would be the typical routine way the majority of workers complete custody reports for courts. This is one disadvantage of more than one social worker being involved in the same custody case.

One distinct advantage of a worker's being able to utilize the methods specified in this manual in evaluation of all parties to a contested custody proceeding would include the following: the recommendation would not just be based on observations and hearsay, but would be based on a worker's first-hand assessment of all the parties in the custody case consisting of the following procedures being utilized: (1) in-person interviews; (2) home visits; (3) data from completed forms; and, (4) observations of interaction of the litigants with the child/children involved. The in-depth assessment would result from a minimum of 14–17 hours of gathering relevant data with a focus on parenting abilities of litigants.

A recommendation should be based on an in-depth assessment of all factors relevant to determining the best interests of a child in a custody case and should not be a recommendation based on a superficial or haphazard assessment. Superficial reasons for recommending that a person have legal custody of a child may include the following: one litigant has a more respected social status than another litigant; one litigant makes a better impression in considering that person's verbal skills whereas the other litigant may be at a disadvantage in not being able to express himself verbally in an effective way, or one of the litigants may be totally illiterate.

In utilizing the completion of forms by litigants, it would be rather unfair to expect the illiterate person to complete written tests or forms unless some provision is made for the litigant's inability to read or write. A person's verbal skills are only one factor to consider along with all the other observations and information. *No one factor should be considered without viewing it in the context of all additional observations, considerations, and information.* No recommendation should be based on only one or two factors involved in the assessment process.

Chapter 8

HYPOTHETICAL EXAMPLE ILLUSTRATING THE VALUE OF A SOCIAL WORKER'S PERSPECTIVE

In conclusion, please consider the following hypothetical example to help illustrate the value of a social worker's assessment of facts. Mr. X has just won $17 million in the Lotto, he is in the process of filing for divorce and wants legal custody of his children. Mr. X has just purchased land where oil has been discovered. Mr. X has been having physical symptoms (no diagnosis yet) but has been told he may need surgery in the near future. Mr. X also has dental problems. Mr. X is very likeable, has many desirable qualities, and plans to marry your daughter after his divorce is finalized. You have never met Mr. X, don't have much information about him, and may not get to meet him until your daughter's wedding day. The following five professionals each have their own perception of Mr. X, all of which are determined to be accurate based on facts. You can only talk to one professional about Mr. X prior to your daughter's wedding. Which professional will you decide to talk to? Here are the first four different professional's perception of Mr. X:

(1) The attorney perceives Mr. X as a potential client that can be represented in a contested custody case and the fact is Mr. X files for custody and asks the attorney to represent him.

(2) An investor perceives that Mr. X might be a potential investor due to the Lotto winnings. Mr. X is approached by the investor and decides to invest $100,000 in a project initiated by the investor.

(3) A dentist perceives Mr. X as a potential patient due to Mr. X's dental problem, approaches Mr. X, and is correct in that Mr. X makes an appointment to get needed dental work done.

(4) A surgeon perceives Mr. X as a potential patient due to Mr. X's need for emergency surgery, approaches Mr. X, and Mr. X has the surgeon schedule him for surgery the following week.

As indicated, all four above professionals found out their perception of Mr. X was correct. Your daughter's wedding to Mr. X is next month.

21

You have to decide which of the five professionals to talk to since you can only talk to one. By the way, the fifth professional is a social worker and the social worker's assessment includes the perceptions of the *a*ttorney, *in*vestor, *d*entist, *s*urgeon and also includes a discussion with a physician. The social worker confirms her initial assessment that Mr. X is diagnosed as having AIDS. Which professional's perception of Mr. X would be the most valuable for you to know?

Figure 2.

A MANUAL ON INVESTIGATING CHILD CUSTODY REPORTS

PART II

REASON FOR PART II OF MANUAL

After utilizing the methods outlined in this manual routinely in my completion of custody investigations, I discovered a need for the addition of practical information (including form letters) which can be utilized to further clarify relevant custody issues. (Please refer to the Appendix section for the complete set of forms to be utilized in all custody investigations.) Workers who expressed an interest in utilizing the methods outlined in Part I of my manual still had some questions including the type of format that was used in a completed report to the court. There is no way to include all information needed to complete custody investigations, but hopefully Part II includes enough practical information that will aid in the investigation being completed in an organized, timely manner.

It might be noted that the methods outlined in Part I of my manual have been utilized (sometimes in modified form) in completing investigations relating to visitation issues regarding custody as well as in completing investigative home studies that are not primarily custody related cases but rather are cases in which court action resulted from child abuse and/or neglect. Some of the cases requiring court-ordered reports resulted from the court action initiated under the Juvenile Court Act. These are also cases in which this manual can be utilized. This author has also utilized methods outlined in this manual in completing predispositional court reports. Some of the forms included in the Appendix section have been entered as evidence in some of the court hearings in custody cases in which this author has testified.

This author's intent is to provide useful practical information that will be beneficial to other social workers or mental health professionals involved in child custody investigations.

Chapter 9

COLLATERALS TO CONSIDER CONTACTING ROUTINELY IN CUSTODY INVESTIGATIONS

(1) Collaterals listed on questionnaire.
(2) Employer (if person currently employed).
(3) Sheriff's Department.
(4) Police Department.
(5) School staff (if school-age children).
(6) Neighbors of Litigants.
(7) Verify source and amount of income.

The above collaterals are routinely contacted in custody investigations as all have the potential for contributing beneficial information about the litigants who might have an effect on a litigant's parenting abilities, emotional stability, dependability and/or pattern of accepting responsibilities. Please refer to the Appendix section for this author's collateral form, verification of employment form, school form and law enforcement form. Utilizing the forms saves a tremendous amount of time and provides written data that is readily accessible in the file if needed during the court hearing. It might be noted that some of the forms have places for the litigants to give written consent for the information to be obtained. Many employers particularly are reluctant to relay information that is really considered confidential. Many professionals also are concerned about potential lawsuits that might be initiated by a litigant if adverse information would voluntarily be given that might contribute to a litigant's difficulty in obtaining legal custody of children.

Chapter 10

THE ROLE OF THE INVESTIGATOR IN CHILD CUSTODY INVESTIGATIONS

The role of the investigator in custody cases is usually an invaluable aid to the court. A mental health professional (such as a counselor, social worker, psychologist or psychiatrist) has a responsibility to complete an objective investigation that includes an investigation of the following:

1. An investigation into the parenting abilities of each litigant (including parental strengths and weaknesses).
2. Investigation into the needs and feelings of the child or children involved.
3. An investigation into the allegations concerning each litigant (especially the allegations that have a direct effect on the child or children).
4. An investigation of each litigant's past parenting abilities, current parenting abilities, and potential for assuming future parenting responsibilities.
5. Investigation of the following criteria as it relates to each litigant

   a. continuity of relationships
   b. the extent of child care involvement of each litigant since the child's birth to the present
   c. quality of child care provided by each litigant
   d. flexibility regarding visitation issues
   e. the encouragement of a positive loving relationship between the child and spouse or ex-spouse
   f. psychological parent
   g. non-judgmental attitude toward others
   h. individualizing needs of the child (focus on child's needs rather than on litigant's needs)
   i. investigation into other factors relating to each litigant such as physical health, emotional health, financial assets, employment

history, marital history, lifestyle, current living arrangements, child rearing philosophy, stability, dependability, relationship of litigants with extended families, etc.

6. Investigation into child's relationships or interactions with each litigant
7. An assessment of each litigant's abilities to be actively involved in providing quality care to a child or children, consisting of care that would adequately meet the child's needs and would not be care that would result in neglect and/or abuse of the child.

The completed investigation should be the end result of obtaining relevant information and observations from *all* litigants, children (if old enough to be interviewed), collaterals, school information (if school-age children are involved), and other relevant information completed by litigants and children.

In summary, a custody investigation is not considered to be thorough or objective unless the investigator has obtained enough information and observations to be able to list parental strengths and weaknesses of each litigant (advantages and disadvantages of each litigant's home). An investigation into all relevant factors related to the best interests of children will provide objective data to aid the court in the important task of determining which litigant can best meet the medical, physical, emotional, religious, and educational needs of the child or children involved in the pending custody litigation. One of the primary goals of the investigator is not just to gather all the relevant data, but it is also essential to analyze the existing data so the numerous pages of data can be condensed into a *concise* report that summarizes the relevant data in terms of major criteria reflected in each litigant's home environment.

If the end result of the investigation furnishes the type of assessment recommended, the court will have at its disposal information that may otherwise not be provided by any other means. *An investigation of each litigant's parental functioning should be a mandatory requirement of court litigation in all contested custody cases. The person who can best assume the responsibilities of the investigator in custody cases is a social worker or other mental health professional who has the specialized knowledge, experience, education, and expertise in the complexities of the custody area. The investigation plays a very important role in custody decisions being based on relevant information directly related to parenting abilities. May the investigator with expertise in the complexities of contested custody be considered to play a vital role in all contested custody litigations, now and in the future.*

Chapter 11

UTILIZATION OF THE FORMS INCLUDED IN THE APPENDIX

This author designed the majority of the forms in the Appendix in 1987 and regularly utilizes all the forms in each custody investigation. It is important that the litigants and children complete each form (with the exception of the questionnaire) in the investigator's presence and that the forms not be sent by mail.

It has been this author's experience that litigants many times will have spouses complete the initial questionnaire (in cases where litigants have remarried) or might consult with an attorney in attempts to obtain help or advice in the best way to answer each question. One particular litigant had his attorney completing the questionnaire. The forms such as the Completion and True-False forms are utilized in helping to assess parenting abilities of litigants as well as the seven major criteria. It is therefore very important that the investigator obtain each litigant's own ideas and feelings. By the forms being completed in the investigator's presence, there is assurance that the litigant is not obtaining any help in completing the forms. Each litigant also has the opportunity to complete the forms in the same manner.

Be sure to have the children complete their own forms if they are old enough to do so. If not old enough or if a litigant is not able to read or write, the questions may be read and the person's exact response to each question can be recorded on the forms. The professional completing the form should sign the form with a statement of the name of the person providing the answers, as well as the date and location where the interview was conducted. It is important that the litigants and children who complete their own forms sign their name on each form and write the date the form was completed.

The value of the above procedures cannot be overemphasized. For example, one litigant testified in court that he assumed the majority of child care responsibilities himself during his marriage. When the author looked at the child care task form he completed during the investigation, his answers clearly indicated that he himself only assumed major child care responsibilities for one or two child care tasks listed and that his ex-wife assumed the majority of the child care responsibilities. Those particular child care task forms completed by the litigants were entered as evidence at the court hearing.

It is difficult for a litigant to dispute his own answers to questions when confronted with the form he obviously completed. The forms have the person's signature so it is difficult to try to say the form does not reflect the litigant's answers.

Obviously, there are no "right" or "wrong" answers as such on the forms, and how one form or one or two questions are answered are not the most important considerations. However, the forms provide additional data that can be analyzed in their entirety, along with answers to interview questions, observations of interactions between each litigant and child, information from collaterals, and all other data available that would be relevant in assessing the major criteria.

Whether or not the forms are answered truthfully can also be assessed. For example, if a litigant answers "false" to the question regarding whether or not he has ever had any problem with alcohol or drugs and then you have documentation that he has been diagnosed by mental health staff as being an alcoholic or has been in an in-patient alcoholic treatment program, there is a good possibility that the litigant's other answers to questions might not be answered honestly and the litigant's credibility would be in question.

Answers to questions on the forms that seem inappropriate should be discussed with the litigant during interviews to try to assess the reason for the answers. Inappropriate answers may be due to inappropriate child rearing philosophy, a lack of understanding of the meaning of the question, a matter of a litigant not reading the question carefully enough, or an answer that seems inappropriate might have an explanation given that would be appropriate within a certain context.

For example, if a child says that he is being followed, it may sound like a possible symptom of paranoia when in fact a child might be followed by a parent or by a person such as a detective hired by one of the parents. Therefore, the child's statement that he is being followed might be very true and factual.

Answers to forms such as the child care task forms completed by litigants may be compared to a child's answers to the child care tasks form for comparison purposes. For example, if a mother indicates her husband virtually assumed no child care responsibilities but the husband and his son both indicate that he was the primary person responsible for child care tasks during the marriage, then it would seem that the mother's answers may not be accurate. This would seem to be the case unless another explanation is available such as the following: the son has a fear of his father due to having been the victim of physical or sexual abuse by the father in the past or the son has a fear of answering questions in a way that would anger his father (even if the end result might be answers that are not accurate) due to the child's fear of being abused by his father in the future.

It should be emphasized that the forms are only one source of data utilized in the assessment phase and should be considered and reviewed in addition to all other data prior to completing the assessment.

Chapter 12

THE IMPORTANCE OF OBSERVING LITIGANTS WITH CHILDREN DURING THE INVESTIGATION

An essential part of the investigation is to observe the interaction of each litigant with the child or children. The observation time should be equal in terms of each litigant's time with the child. This observation of interaction is especially essential when pre-school age children are involved in the custody case as the investigator does not have the advantage of being able to interview the child.

If a child is being "brainwashed" by one of the litigants, this can usually become evident during the observation process. For example, consider the following hypothetical case in which a four year old child (whose father has temporary legal custody of her) immediately begins making negative statements to her mother the minute she visits her mother. Statements are made by the little girl to her mother such as: "You have upset me too much already" when in actuality the mother did not do or say anything that would seem to be upsetting. When the child makes negative statements to the mother such as "You only want custody of me so you can get Public Aid," it is almost certain the child is repeating statements she has heard her father saying.

A child may say that he or she will play with the one parent if that parent promises he or she won't tell the other parent. This again reflects a child's wanting to interact in a positive way with the parent but not wanting to do this if the other parent would find out. The child may believe a parent would consider the child to be disloyal if he is "kind to the enemy," so to speak. In this case, the enemy referred to is the litigant who has *not* brainwashed the child. The above examples can be indications of "brainwashing" of the child being done by the parent who has temporary custody of the child.

Observation of interaction between a parent and child might result in the following observations: a parent's responding very appropriately and affectionately to a child, reflecting a sensitivity to and understanding of the needs of the child and demonstrating an ability to focus on the child's needs. This same litigant might not be very skilled at verbalizing this understanding of the child's needs. Another litigant might be very skilled in verbalizing and be very persuasive in an interview situation. This same person during an interaction with the child might demonstrate behavior reflecting lack of patience with the child, unrealistic expectations of the child, and behavior that reflects more of a tolerance of time with the child rather than a genuine enjoyment of opportunities to interact with a child.

The amount of spontaneity a litigant demonstrates toward the child, the quality of the interaction (both verbally and non-verbally) between each litigant and child, and the extent of interaction between them provide further data to utilize in the assessment phase.

A child (especially a pre-school age child) will typically provide information given in a spontaneous way and some of the information may be significant since the child is usually too young to really comprehend the implications of some of the information. For example, if a four year old blurts out that he or she would really like to visit his daddy but his mommy won't let him because his daddy won't pay child support like he is supposed to, it may be quite clear that the mother is not focusing on the child's love of his father and need to spend time with the father. Instead, the mother is focusing on her own anger and resentment of not receiving financial assistance from her spouse or ex-spouse.

This author would definitely agree that a litigant has a responsibility to pay child support if financially able to do so, but the child's needs should still be given primary consideration. If a child loves both parents and benefits with interaction from the father, then the mother should permit visitation regardless of whether or not child support is paid.

It should be stressed that the responsibility of a litigant to pay child support if financially in a position to do so should equally be the responsibility of both parents. If a child is residing with the father since the parent's separation and the mother is employed, she has just as much of a responsibility to pay child support as the father would if the situation were reversed. The examples are applicable to the father if the situation is reversed, the father has custody, and the mother fails to pay court-ordered child support.

In summary, observations of interactions have the potential of providing insights that might not be revealed in the absence of the observation.

Chapter 13

THE ASSESSMENT PHASE OF THE CUSTODY INVESTIGATION

The assessment phase of the custody investigation is completed prior to dictating the final written report to the court. It is the end result of the following: hours of interviewing litigants and children; observing interaction of litigants with children; observing each litigant's home environment; reviewing relevant social history of each litigant; obtaining relevant information from collaterals (such as neighbors, relatives, employers, law enforcement staff and school staff); and reviewing all the forms completed by litigants, children and/or collaterals. It typically takes a minimum of three to four hours to complete the assessment in a typical custody case.

In the assessment, it is important to list advantages and disadvantages to the child or children if the child or children resided with each litigant on a permanent basis. In other words, the report should mention positives and negatives of each litigant and should not be one sided. Usually at the completion of the assessment, it is evident that one litigant has more advantages than disadvantages, and the other litigant would typically have more disadvantages than advantages. This author can only recall approximately two custody cases which resulted in each litigant having an equal number of advantages and disadvantages.

The advantages and disadvantages should primarily relate to the seven major criteria listed in this manual. The forms as well as interview questions were designed to help assess the seven major criteria. The investigative process viewed in its entirety should result in a total picture at the end that reflects which litigant's home environment meets the majority of the seven major criteria.

Without the type of thorough investigation that is recommended in this manual, it is not possible to assess all the criteria in a thorough manner. After all, the more data available, the better chance the assessment will be accurate. Consider a physician's diagnosis based on one ten-minute examination versus an examination that includes an upper GI, lower GI, blood tests, urinalysis and x-rays. This would be analogous to an investigator's completing a superficial "home study" collection of information versus completing a thorough investigation that includes the following: a minimum of 14 to 17 hours of interviews, observations and data collecting that is focused on the following: investigating parenting abilities of litigants, needs of the children, and investigation of which of the seven major criteria would apply to each litigant's home.

A true custody investigation is just that—an *investigation* that involves hours of thorough documentation of relevant information and observations focused on the major criteria. Superficial factors such as a physical description of a litigant's home, employment history, marital history, income, etc., all usually have little direct relationship to parenting abilities, although the information may be indicative of other strengths or weaknesses of the litigant.

Gathering all the data in a custody investigation is time consuming, but the most difficult aspect of the investigative process is the analysis and assessment of all the volumes of pages of notes and forms in each case. The assessment phase is certainly the most important part of the investigation and should hopefully be one of the most beneficial aspects to the court, litigants, and children, particularly if the assessment is based on accurate documentation of available facts.

A custody report without a thorough assessment would be about as useful as an air-conditioner in a home without electricity. In summary, complete the assessment phase very carefully and accurately and be sure it is based on enough relevant factual data to document the information contained in the assessment.

If completed properly, the assessment should be to a custody report like a completed "Mona Lisa" painting would be to an artist. The assessment would be like the "frosting" on a cake. If done properly, the assessment will be a significant contribution to the information available to the court prior to a final custody decision being made. The importance of the assessment cannot be overemphasized and needs to be understood completely by any professional completing a custody investigation.

Chapter 14

ASSESSMENT OF THE SEVEN MAJOR CRITERIA

Assessing the seven major criteria takes several hours of analyzing all data available in each case. There may be as many as one hundred pages of notes and forms to review, including notes from observing interactions of litigants and children, observations made during home visits, and other relevant data. It was only after completing research and almost two years of specialization in the custody area that this author began formulating the actual principles into a specific list of criteria that seem to be the most essential to consider. After determining the major criteria to look for, then the forms were designed to help provide data that would correlate with each criteria.

The criteria of flexibility regarding visitation issues has relevant data that can be obtained and analyzed from the following: the form with questions for litigants; completion forms; true-false forms; information from collaterals; and by interviewing litigants and children. This criteria is especially important because children usually benefit most by being able to spend quality time with each parent. Some parents intentionally try to sabotage a non-custodial parent's visits with a child. A parent who tries to interfere with visits has decreased his parental assets and is usually not focusing on the needs of the child but instead is being self-centered.

The criteria of being non-judgmental and encouraging the child to have a positive relationship with the other parent is a criteria that seems to complement the one above. The same forms and interview questions can assess the presence or absence of these criteria. A litigant who does not demonstrate the above two criteria certainly decreases his or her parental assets.

Individualizing needs of children is one of the criteria that seems to at least partly go "hand in hand" with the two previous criteria. Unless there are facts to substantiate that a child cannot benefit by visits or a positive relationship with the non-custodial parent, then for a litigant to not recognize this benefit to the child and be able to place the child's needs first is an example of *not* individualizing needs of children. Some-times it is difficult or virtually impossible for many litigants to demon-strate that this particular criteria is present in their home environment. A parent significantly compromises his or her parenting abilities if the parent tries to "brainwash" a child against the other parent or tries to make the child feel guilty or disloyal if he wants to spend time with the other parent. Many children even feel guilty if they are actually looking forward to visits with the other parent.

The criteria *continuity of relationships* can be assessed by questions in interviews. This author would define "continuity of relationships" as being a continuity or continuation of relationships and emotional attach-ments between a child and parent or parent substitute over an extended period of time. The importance to the child in this criteria being present is emphasized by many of the experts in the custody area. Sometimes there is such a delay from the date of the temporary custody hearing to the final hearing. A parent who obtained temporary legal custody of a child may not have the best parenting abilities but if the child is in that parent's custody for one year or longer, it might be very disruptive to the child emotionally if this continuity of relationships is broken or terminated.

The criteria relating to quantity of child care involvement can be assessed partly by the child care task forms. Both parents may be spend-ing time with the child but it is certainly important to assess which parent assumed the greatest responsibility for child care tasks such as the following: taking the child to medical appointments; attending school functions with the child; taking care of the child when he is sick; handling emergencies that arise; and, taking greater responsibility for other child care tasks (assuming one parent spent a greater amount of time than the other in this area). This criteria is assessed from the time of each child's birth to the present time.

The criteria "psychological parent" would be defined by this author as the parent or parent figure that the child consistently has demonstrated (either by behavior and/or verbally) the greatest emotional attachment. In other words, the psychological parent for a child is the parent, parent substitute, or parent figure with whom the child has the greatest emo-tional attachment and has formed the greatest emotional bond. If the child's emotional attachment seems to be equal toward each parent, then each parent would be considered to be a psychological parent for the child. The completion forms for children in addition to a child's answers to interview questions and observations of interactions can all help assess this criteria.

In this author's experience, most children are more emotionally attached to one parent than the other and reflect this attachment in their answers to questions as well as in their behavior toward each litigant. Children further usually will not hesitate to give their preference regarding the permanent living arrangements they desire. The child's preference is usually always predictable and consistent based on other answers to questions on the forms and in answers to interview questions.

It is very understandable that currently, it seems that women may obtain permanent legal custody of children more often than men. When one realizes that in the majority of cases, it is usually the mother who assumes responsibility for the majority of child care tasks, is the psychological parent, and meets the continuity of relationships criteria, then the mother's obtaining custody would seem quite logical. Most women obtain temporary legal custody of the child and/or are the ones who usually provide daily care for the child after a separation or divorce. If the mother is the one who spends the most time with the child, assumes responsibility for most of the child care tasks, and is the primary one who sits up at night with a child when a child is sick, comforts the child when the child is upset, and handles crises involving the child, then it would be logical to assume that it would be understandable why the child would be the most attached emotionally to the mother. If mothers, as a general rule, meet the above three or more of the seven major criteria and the child is emotionally attached to the mother, then it would seem logical and understandable why mothers frequently would and should obtain permanent legal custody of children.

It has been this author's experience that many fathers possess several of the above major criteria and are recommended for custody if they have more of the seven major criteria than the mother. Fathers have obtained permanent legal custody of the children in cases when it was appropriate. In the final analysis, it is not the gender that is important but which litigant and litigant's environment contains the majority of the seven major criteria.

The quality of child care criteria is one that is important to assess and one that probably requires more subjective judgment on the part of the investigator than the others. In considering the quality of care, the total picture needs to be viewed and not just one or two isolated incidents or examples. Some of the criteria such as individualizing needs of the child overlap with the quality criteria. Although it is important that a parent spend time with a child, the quality of time is certainly crucial. If a parent is physically with the child all day but takes virtually no time to be actively involved with the child in constructive activities, then the quantity of time criteria loses some of the potential benefits. A parent who realistically has limited time to spend with a child but spends the time in being actively involved in educational activities with the child, demonstrates some of the reasons the quality factor might be much more important to the child than the amount of time that is spent with the child. A child who loves to play ball and hates to fish would in all probability enjoy a few hours of playing ball with a parent much more than spending an entire day fishing with the other parent.

Try to focus on a child's needs as much as possible. Realistically, there are times when a parent has to engage in activities that are not child-oriented; however, choices can be made that also take into consideration the needs of the child. For example, in this author's completion of this manual as well as the needed revisions, numerous hours were devoted to this goal. One time chosen to complete the above goal was to begin writing after my husband's and my son went to bed at night even though this meant my staying up until 3:00 A.M. numerous evenings. Other times selected were days when I took my son to Show-Biz Pizza (sometimes for four hours at a time). My son thoroughly enjoys playing with other children at Show-Biz Pizza so I could easily devote time to writing my book while my son played and at least we were together. *Realistic goals can be achieved without totally ignoring the needs of the child.*

In summary, some answers to questions on the forms in the Appendix might have implications for more than one of the seven major criteria. All the interviews, forms completed, observations, and relevant information from collaterals all work together toward providing a total picture of the major criteria present in each litigant's home. The above procedures viewed in their entirety as a total picture seem to place a custody dispute in its proper perspective.

Chapter 15

COMPLETED CUSTODY INVESTIGATION INFORMATION

A completed custody investigation includes the following information:

(1) Completed questionnaires returned by the litigants.
(2) Interviews of litigants.
(3) Interviews of children (if 5 years or older).
(4) Interviews of collaterals.
(5) Observations during home visits.
(6) Observations of children's interactions with each litigant.
(7) Forms completed by litigants, children and/or relevant collaterals.
(8) Assessment of parenting abilities of each litigant.
(9) Conclusion or recommendations.

It might be noted that a copy of the questionnaire completed by each litigant is included with this author's typed court report which routinely is sent to the appropriate judge as well as the attorneys involved in the case (including the attorney who represents the children if one is involved). If a litigant does not have an attorney representing him, then, by law in Illinois, he is to be sent a copy of the court report directly. The additional forms completed by litigants, children, and/or collaterals are not shown to anyone unless a judge or attorney requests to see the file. The forms are kept as part of the file and are utilized in the review of information that is completed during the assessment phase of the investigation.

Chapter 16

EXAMPLE OF MAIN INFORMATION AND HEADINGS INCLUDED IN COMPLETED REPORT TO THE COURT

Investigative Custody Report

(1) Docket number.

(2) County of court jurisdiction.

(3) Each litigant's name and address.

(4) Names and birthdates of the children involved in the custody proceedings.

(5) Opening statement including court date if date of hearing is scheduled.

"This report is submitted in accordance with an order of the court to investigate both parties relative to the custody of two minor children. To this worker's knowledge, no date has been set for a hearing in regard to this matter."

(6) Method utilized in completing Investigative Custody Report.

(7) Worker's contacts with litigants.

(8) Contacts with collaterals.

(9) Significant information obtained during interviews with children.

(10) Significant information obtained during interviews with litigants (including allegations, if any).

(11) Significant information obtained from collaterals.

(12) Observations during home visits.

(13) Observations of children's interaction with each litigant.

(14) Worker's assessment.

(15) Conclusion. Don't forget to include copies of the completed questionnaires with your final court report.

Chapter 17

SEVEN HINTS TO UTILIZE IN COMPLETING CUSTODY INVESTIGATIONS

The following are suggestions that I have found are extremely beneficial in conducting custody investigations. I, therefore, would like to share the ideas in hopes that other professionals may benefit from these seven hints. While completing any custody investigation, it is important to consider the following during all aspects of the investigation, while on-going services are provided (if any), and during the court hearing if you testify.

(1) *Always* remain as objective as it is humanly possible to be.

(2) *Always obtain both sides of the custody issue*, realizing that each litigant may seem to be equally convincing in presenting their concerns. It is quite common for a worker to have ambivalent feelings regarding the issues presented after hearing both sides of issues.

(3) Keep accurate notes on the content of each interview at the time each interview is being conducted.

(4) Keep all handwritten notes as copies of those notes may be requested by one or more attorneys involved in the custody litigation.

(5) Be sure to document the time each interview with each litigant and child begins and the time each interview is terminated. Be sure to include the dates of each interview and the location of the interview.

(6) Keep in mind that not all judges are receptive to written recommendations; however, if assessments are written in a thorough and accurate manner and supported by documentation at the court hearing, then the best plan for the children will seem quite obvious unless the litigant's parenting abilities are almost equal and/or the benefits to the children provided by each litigant are almost equal.

(7) *Always be flexible in viewing custody issues and be open to new ideas.* Custody cases are usually quite complex and there is usually never any "easy solution"! Each investigation provides an opportunity to gain more experience, understanding, knowledge, skill, and appreciation for

the exciting area of contested custody. Professional growth should be an on-going process that never remains static. In closing, if it is at all feasible, take advantage of being an active professional participant in the exciting four C's!!!

     C ontested
     C hild
     C ustody
     C hallenge

A MANUAL ON INVESTIGATING CHILD CUSTODY REPORTS

PART III

A Focus on Relevant Custody Issues

REASONS FOR PART III OF MANUAL

After writing the manual on the completion of custody investigations, relevant custody issues have been brought to this author's attention and each area of concern was deemed important enough to warrant individualized attention. The first issue or area of concern centers around the importance of professional social workers not only being involved in completing custody investigations for courts, but also the possibility of legislation being changed in the future in order to legally prevent courts from utilizing the option of ordering the involvement of Department of Children and Family Services professional social workers in the completion of custody investigations. If courts did not have the option to order Department of Children and Family Services involvement in custody cases, the end result would be an injustice to children involved in custody litigation (in this worker's opinion). In fact, it is particularly beneficial if more than one professional (such as a psychologist or social worker) can be involved in the same custody investigation or evaluation. The first article addresses this issue.

The second area of concern involves the misconceptions surrounding the phrase "home study" or the potential benefit of utilizing terms such as "custody investigation" or "investigative report" instead of the term "home study." Many people (professionals included) have no real understanding of what a thorough custody investigation should entail. The second article relates to this issue.

The third area of concern involves the importance of considering *all* factors in determining the plan that would be in a child's best interest. A consideration of *all* factors would certainly include a recognition of the importance of a parent-child relationship and the potential tragedy that could result if legal rights are ignored such as a child's right to be raised in the home of a parent unless there are facts to substantiate that this plan is not in the best interests of a child. Even though this author's articles include hypothetical examples, it must be noted that *all articles are based on the research and first-hand experience that this author has in the specialized area of contested custody.* Therefore, the *hypothetical examples have sufficient factual basis to warrant serious consideration of the information and implications contained in the third part of this author's manual.* Other relevant custody

51

issues are discussed in this section, in addition to the above three areas of concern.

The inclusion of the chapters (written mostly in article form) are meant to supplement information contained in Part I and Part II of the manual this author wrote. In this author's opinion, it would be most beneficial to any professional involved in the area of contested custody litigation to read the contents of all three parts of this manual in its entirety in order to obtain the most complete picture of the process of completing a thorough objective custody investigation, taking into consideration *all* factors that would relate to the best interests of a child.

In essence, all three parts of this author's manual are interrelated and should be viewed in its entirety in order to be certain that all major factors related to the best interests of a child are considered during the investigative process. This author's goal is to continue writing in the contested custody area and, therefore, more articles may be included in the future.

Some of the issues discussed in this section are issues that many professionals who are not directly involved in the custody area, would have minimal understanding of in terms of the importance, relevance and significance of the information. A professional without specialized knowledge and experience in the custody area would have about as much expertise, appreciation for, and understanding of the complexities in contested child custody litigation as a proctologist would have expertise and experience in performing delicate, tedious brain surgery. Another illustration or analogy would be an expert sky diver who has never gone swimming in his entire life and has a phobia about being in the water, but yet he begins to criticize diving techniques of diving instructors who have noticeable expertise in diving and swimming techniques.

It cannot be overemphasized or stressed that it is wise for professionals to be critical of only those areas of which they have the knowledge base, experience, and expertise to understand. One would not want to have to depend on a person to teach a subject as important as AIDS prevention by a person who has not read the first pamphlet or book on AIDS or has no factual knowledge base about this subject. Don't children who are innocent victims of custody litigation deserve and have a right to services provided by a professional with expertise in the custody area? After all, children have their entire future at stake and will be affected significantly by court decisions. If you were in that child's position, would you rather place your trust in a professional with expertise in the custody area or a professional with minimal or no real interest or understanding in the complexities of contested custody?

Some professionals have the mistaken misconception that specialization is needed in areas of investigating abuse or neglect allegations, providing sexual abuse treatment to perpetrators of sexual abuse, licensing and other areas of child welfare, but not in the area of contested child custody. *This author cannot think of one logical explanation for the above philosophy.* This author is a Hospice volunteer and in order to be eligible and accepted as a Hospice volunteer, a volunteer *must* complete a minimal number of training sessions as well as completing required on-going training. It is not logical to believe that an area as important as custody would not require more specialized training than would be required of volunteers.

Your ideas regarding custody issues are important because in the future you yourself, your child, your grandchild or someone you know may be depending on services by the persons you decide are the most capable of rendering custody services. Be sure you realize the implications of your choice, particularly as the children affected by professional involvement in custody litigation deserve consideration of all issues that have the potential of having a significant impact on their future.

Figure 3. Children who are in the middle of a contested custody proceedings have rights too. One of these rights is the right to professional services which will help enable them to live in the most nurturing environment possible. Children who are the innocent victims in a contested custody proceedings have a right to court-ordered investigations and evaluations being provided by professionals who have specialized knowledge and expertise in the custody area.

Chapter 18

DOES ANYONE CARE?

Consider this hypothetical situation. Mr. and Mrs. X are currently in the middle of a contested custody dispute involving their three year old daughter, Amanda. Mrs. X has been emotionally abusive to Amanda and has neglected her since her birth, although no one made an official report to State Central Registry so that the alleged neglect could be investigated. The child's father has assumed the major child care responsibilities since the child's birth and the child is emotionally attached to the father but is not considered old enough to give credible information. The mother's relatives are wealthy and are giving her money to hire the best divorce and custody attorney available. The father has recently been laid off from work and receives unemployment benefits, but these benefits do not amount to enough money to pay the $1000 retainer fee for legal representation. The father's relatives are not financially in a position to pay attorney fees for Mr. X. Mrs. X is also very articulate and has a talent for telling lies in such a way that many persons would be "conned" by her fabrications. Mr. X is not very articulate and is not outspoken.

Whose responsibility is it to consider the best interests of this three year old child? Since no official report has been called in to State Central Registry, Division of Child Protection staff will not be investigating the child's situation. Even if an official report is made to the Hotline and an indicated neglect report results, in many areas the situation may not be considered serious enough that the state's attorney will file a petition, although years of repeated emotional abuse and physical neglect are bound to have a detrimental effect on the child. If follow up services are provided by agency staff from Department of Children and Family Services or other agency staff, the end result may be similar to many families who have received services from more than one agency, including Department of Children and Family Services, and still make no significant change in their lifestyle and who continue to exhibit a pattern of neglectful or abusive behavior toward children.

The contested custody area provides an opportunity for an assessment of parenting abilities of litigants by professional Department of Children and Family Services staff under the current Marriage and Dissolution of Marriage Act. But what if that option were no longer available to the courts? The end result may be a judge granting permanent legal custody to the mother due to lack of documentation assessing parenting abilities of the litigants involved. Since the child involved is too young to provide testimony at the hearing, the judge is faced with one person's word against the other.

Typical testimony during a custody hearing will seldom be testimony that provides documentable information regarding parenting abilities, as would a thorough assessment by a professional with skills in assessing environmental factors relating to the best interests of a child. An opportunity to aid the court with significant information that could make a difference in terms of the final custody decision may be lost if current legislation is changed in regard to a court's authority to order Department of Children and Family Services involvement in providing an investigation and report to the court that will relate to all factors involving the best interests of the child.

Many courts do not have any person within the court system who can provide investigations and reports in custody cases. If psychological evaluations are too costly for litigants, then this option is not available. If Department of Children and Family Services' mission is truly "based on a recognition and conviction that children must have a consistent, nurturing environment in order to grow physically and psychologically," as indicated in the Department of Children and Family Services' Child Welfare Services Practice Handbook, then why should an opportunity be lost to be involved in an actual case pending in court and one in which Department of Children and Family Services professional involvement may really make a difference in this three year old child's life?

It seems that this child and others involved in contested custody deserve intervention from professional staff, especially considering the fact that this intervention has a definite possibility of resulting in a court decision in which the adult that obtains permanent legal custody of the child will be the adult with the best parenting abilities and not the adult who is the least likely to provide a home environment—one in which the child might be neglected, physically or sexually abused, and/or emotionally damaged.

In summary, the custody area is one that can be viewed in the following two ways: (1) an area that Department of Children and Family Services professionals should find a legal way to avoid the responsibility of making a beneficial contribution to the children, litigants, and courts, even knowing in reality the end result in all probability will be no professional involvement in the custody area and complex decisions made without judges having the benefit of objective information as to parenting abilities of litigants; or (2) the opportunity for Department of Children and Family Services staff to provide professional services that can result in children being allowed, through legal channels, to live in the most nurturing environment possible.

Please take a moment to reflect on Department of Children and Family Services's mission and emphasis on "protecting and promoting the welfare of *all* children." Can you honestly *not care* about the future of children who are in the complex situation of being in the middle of contested custody? Can you answer this three year old child's question: *"Does anyone care?"* The hypothetical example is typical of custody situations that end up daily in our court system.

Just assume for one minute that you are not only one of the litigants in a contested custody case but also the litigant with the best parenting abilities; yet you may be in a position of losing custody of your child. Let's hope for your sake and the sake of your child that there are professional Department of Children and Family Services employees who care enough to respond "yes" to this child's question. Again, I ask the question, "Does anyone care?" If your answer is "yes" to Amanda's question, please be actively involved in efforts to oppose any legislative change that would *not* give courts the authority to order Department of Children and Family Services' involvement in custody cases. I'm sure Amanda will thank you, and so will many other children involved in this complex contested custody area.

Chapter 19

"HOME STUDY" VERSUS "INVESTIGATIVE REPORT"

When a court order is sent to the Department of Children and Family Services with the order specifying that Department of Children and Family Services is ordered to complete a home study, there are varying perceptions of what the home study should include. The typical home study would include information relating to the following areas: family composition (names, birthdates, and birthplaces of family members involved in the court action); current living arrangement; education of each adult member of the household and each school age child; health of each family member; employment; income, marital history of litigants; interests and activities of family members; religious preference; court involvement of any member of the household (court convictions or charges, if any); ideas regarding child rearing including discipline methods advocated and/or utilized; and, information from collaterals. A school report is included for school age children in custody investigations. The above areas are usually covered in all adoptive studies, home studies, or custody investigations.

In a custody investigation, usually a few sentences may be included to indicate a child's preference regarding his permanent living arrangement if the child is old enough to be interviewed and is interviewed by the social worker. Rarely will the statement of preference include more than the child's stated preference. If a thorough assessment is not completed by a social worker, then the interview with the child will not include whether the child's preference is based on facts that would relate to the best interests of the child or whether it is based on facts that in an assessment would relate to information detrimental to the physical and emotional well-being of the child. It would certainly be extremely important to know whether or not a child's preference is based on (1) a litigant's providing the best quality of care that adequately meets the child's physical, emotional, educational, medical, and spiritual needs or (2) based on facts such as the following: the litigant does not supervise the child adequately, lets the child stay up late, even on school nights, the

58

child is exposed to physical violence and/or excessive alcohol and drug usage by adults, or the litigant sets virtually no limits on the type of behavior the child is able to exhibit without any discipline being administered or any negative consequences being imposed by the child's parent or parent substitute. *It should never be forgotten that a child's preference in regard to a living situation is not always based on facts that would be in the child's best interests.* A child's preference is important to convey or consider (provided the child is at least 5 years old), but it is much more important to try to assess reasons for the preference.

If a home study is ordered in a custody case, some people have the misconception that the home study will consist only of a social worker's going to each litigant's home and looking over the physical surroundings as if a comparison would be made as to which litigant can offer the most material advantages to the children or the most expensive house. Some litigants have even thought that no interview was needed by the social worker with the litigants, children, or collaterals and that the social worker could be shown through the house by anyone (even a person with no involvement in the court case). With this perspective, a social worker's looking through each litigant's house for ten minutes is thought to be all the home study will include by many persons including litigants, professionals, and lay persons. This type of thinking is the main reason this author believes that the term "home study" is misleading in terms of the anticipated end result of a judge's ordering a home study. Do most judges really prefer that the report to the court include: (1) a physical description of each litigant's home only (which could be accomplished just as easily by a realtor because the realtor could have an idea of the value of each litigant's house as well) or (2) a report reflecting the following:

    a. A description of each litigant's living arrangement;

    b. An assessment of each litigant's parenting abilities;

    c. An assessment of the quality of child care each litigant has provided in the past as well as currently;

    d. The amount of time each litigant spends in assuming child care responsibilities and in recreational and educational activities with children in the past and currently;

    e. A child's preference regarding his permanent living arrangement if the child is 5 years old or older;

    f. An assessment of the reasons for the child's preference if a preference is expressed;

g. Summary of information from collaterals that would relate to each litigant's parenting abilities;

h. Background information of each litigant covering areas already summarized earlier in this article such as income, employment, marital status, etc.;

i. An assessment of the main factors relating to the best interests of children.

Which type of report would be the most beneficial to the court, the litigants, and, particularly, to the children who are involved in a contested custody situation?

It has been this worker's experience in my specialization of completing custody investigations, that the term "home study" is viewed literally by many people and the term implies that a person's home or house will be studied rather than the adults and children involved in the court action.

It would seem that there would be definite advantages to utilizing the term "*investigative* home study," "investigative report" or "custody investigation" rather than the term "home study." If the social worker completes an investigation that includes a thorough assessment of parenting abilities of litigants and an assessment of the most important factors relating to the best interests of children, then the term "custody investigation" in custody cases or "investigative report" in routine home studies would more accurately describe the end result of what ordering Department of Children and Family Services' involvement is intended to accomplish.

In summary, it would be advantageous to substitute the word "custody investigation" or "investigative report" for "home study" in court orders particularly in custody cases. The end result may be a better quality report which will actually be the result of a thorough investigation of parenting abilities, quality of care of children provided by litigants, and assessment of all major factors related to the best interests of the child rather than a report reflecting only information that could be provided just as easily by the litigant's completing a questionnaire and bringing pictures of each room of their house. It is this author's contention that the more beneficial a report is to the court, the more likely there would be an increase in court orders involving our agency. After all, why would a judge want to order a report or an attorney file a motion for the judge to order a report if the end result would be a report without relevant information. It is almost certain that a professional who completes a report lacking beneficial information would not be expected to testify at a court hearing. *A report that is virtually useless in aiding the court in decision-making would certainly not be missed by anyone involved in a custody case.*

Social workers are in a unique position due to their knowledge and skills in assessing the physical, emotional, and environmental factors relating to the best interests of children, to make a valuable contribution to the contested child custody area. Social workers who are employed by the Department of Children and Family Services are also in the especially unique position of having specialized training in the areas of assessing neglect, physical abuse, sexual abuse, and emotional abuse or neglect of children.

Since it has been this social worker's experience that many custody cases involve alleged abuse or neglect of children by litigants or adult caretakers, a Department of Children and Family Services social worker's knowledge and skills in this specialized area of assessing allegations involving abuse or neglect of children is valuable. After all, if one really considers the best interests of a child in a custody issue, it is essential to view each child with his or her own unique feelings, needs, and ideas within the context of the child's total environment offered by each litigant (including each litigant's extent of parental involvement in addition to the child's home environment, community, and educational or enrichment opportunities offered by each litigant). Any complete assessment takes into consideration all relevant factors. A custody issue is usually always very complex and it is not just one factor that is important, but it is viewing the total picture of the child in his situation in each litigant's home environment that is needed in each custody case pending in court.

In closing, when a court order reflects that a written report is requested from Department of Children and Family Services, consider if you want the end result to be a literal "home study" or an actual "investigative report" that should be part of any custody investigation. If an investigative report is expected or preferred, then it might be beneficial to try to utilize phrases that are less misleading and which more accurately reflect the actual meaning of what the expectations are.

Hopefully the expectations when ordering a report would be that the completed report would be a better quality report based on a *thorough investigation and assessment* or, in essence, a *"custody investigation"* or *"investigative report."*

Chapter 20

"IN A CHILD'S BEST INTEREST"
—BUT FROM WHOSE PERSPECTIVE?

In all contested custody cases, a judge makes a final decision regarding which permanent plan will be in the best interests of the child or children involved in a custody proceeding, considering the options available. It certainly sounds like any decision regarding a child should consider the child's best interest. The only problem is that people have varied opinions and perceptions of exactly what is meant by the phrase "in a child's best interest." If a person attempts to obtain a complete picture of *all* factors involved in a custody case and if a plan doesn't totally disregard basic rights a child has, then the plan should be based on sound judgment. Considering all factors includes assessment of a parent's current parenting abilities in addition to the parent's age, experience in child rearing, potential for parenting abilities, and the parent's motivation to learn successful parenting skills, especially if only one parent is involved in the custody litigation and other persons are grandparents or other relatives of the child in the custody proceeding. But what if "expert witnesses" who provide custody evaluations do not place any importance or totally disregard some of a child's basic rights, such as a child's right to be raised by a parent on a daily basis, unless there is a legitimate reason this is not possible or not recommended? The end result could be disastrous and tragic for the child as well as the parents.

As a means of illustration, let's consider the following hypothetical example. This hypothetical example is based on an actual custody case that this author was involved in, not only in completing more than one investigative report, but in providing testimony at the custody hearing. The actual court decision in this case is currently being appealed. Faith is a two year old girl who is the daughter of a nineteen year old couple. Tragically, Faith's mother is killed in a car accident which leaves Faith's dad, Stan Hope, with the child care responsibilities. Stan is unskilled, unemployed, and currently depends on financial assistance from the

Department of Public Aid. Stan loves Faith very deeply and wants the responsibility and privilege of raising his daughter. As the majority of teenagers Stan's age, he did not have any opportunity to attend parenting classes in school since none were offered, he is immature in many ways and obviously he is not financially secure. He also lacks the stability and emotional maturity and insight of most older persons who have had the opportunity, experience, and ability to learn parenting skills. It should also be noted that Faith has symptoms of wheezing and coughing for which she is obtaining medical attention by Stan's family doctor.

Stan's well-meaning aunt and uncle, Mr. and Mrs. Righteous, decide to visit Stan since they haven't seen him in several years, and their four children are all successful married career persons with children of their own. Mr. and Mrs. Righteous are millionaires, have been married 25 years, and recently received the annual award for "Parents of the Year" which illustrates their excellent parenting abilities. After a week's visit, Mrs. Righteous decides that Faith needs to be in a home environment that offers stability, financial security, both a mother and father figure in the home, and other advantages such as their home offers. Certainly if a person compares the advantages to Faith of Stan's home and the advantages of the Righteous home, one could quickly conclude that it would be in Faith's best interest if Mr. and Mrs. Righteous obtained permanent legal custody of her.

Therefore, Mrs. Righteous files for legal custody of Faith by virtue of her excellent parenting skills, maturity, emotional stability, insight into developmental needs of children, financial situation, and her and her husband's ability to do well on psychological tests administered as part of many custody evaluations.

Mrs. Jan Righteous also alleges in the petition for custody that Faith has been neglected by Stan (lack of adequate medical care), without bothering to obtain the medical opinion of Faith's physician. Faith's physician could easily verify his tentative diagnosis of asthma for which appropriate medical treatment not only has been prescribed by him, but in his opinion, Stan has followed through with administering Faith's medication as prescribed.

The judge did order that a custody evaluation be completed by Dr. Eve Keys (psychologist) who, after completing her observations, interviews, and testing of Mr. and Mrs. Righteous, Stan, and Faith, not only recommends that Mr. and Mrs. Righteous be awarded permanent legal custody of Faith, but also in Dr. Keys's opinion, Mr. and Mrs. Righteous are *the only* acceptable choices for Faith. Let's try to analyze the options available to the judge.

First of all, the best interests of a child in a custody case involving two parents must include a consideration of which parent has the best parenting skills, provided the parent with the best parenting skills is also in a position to provide a home environment that adequately meets a child's physical, educational, medical, spiritual, and emotional needs and an environment where the child is not subjected to abuse or neglect. However, if the options available include one parent of a child and other relatives such as an aunt and uncle, let's not minimize the importance of a child's right to be raised with a parent unless there are *facts* to substantiate that the child would be abused, neglected, or at risk of harm if the child resides with the parent.

After all, the Department of Children and Family Services is not even able by law to sever the parental rights of a parent who has abused or neglected a child in the majority of cases. Abusive and neglectful parents who have children removed from their home can eventually regain legal and physical custody of the child in most cases if there is evidence that the parent has corrected the conditions that were the basis for the child's removal in the first place. After all, many parents who demonstrate excellent parenting abilities currently may be former abusive or neglectful parents or may have exhibited immature behavior, lack of insight, and other qualities in the past that are quite evident in many teenagers or young adults.

For the purposes of this article, let's assume the judge in our hypothetical example decides to take the advice and recommendation of the "expert witness"—psychologist, Dr. Eve Keys. Dr. Keys was one of the witnesses who testified at the custody hearing. The judge awards permanent legal custody of Faith to Mr. and Mrs. Righteous. Just imagine the implications of the above decision.

In considering the best interests of a child in a custody case, it is this author's understanding that a person can file for custody of any child whether related or non-related to a child. Just think of all the teenage parents, widows, widowers, parents who are unemployed, parents receiving financial assistance from the Department of Public Aid, and parents with marital, alcohol, drug-related, or other problems. The above parents could be almost 99% sure that if well-meaning empathetic people such as Mr. and Mrs. Righteous file for legal custody of their children, most categories of parents listed above can be assured that they will not only lose permanent legal custody of their children, but also will never have the opportunity to learn the skills and gain the experience to achieve a goal of becoming a successful parent in the future. Foster parents, couples on adoptive waiting lists, and persons with an educational background in psychology (particularly persons studying psychological testing) can be confident that they have an excellent chance of becoming "instant parents" by just filing for custody of a parent's child or children—provided you select the parent who in all probability would not do as well in a custody evaluation.

In the future, it might even be possible to build courthouses next to maternity wards to facilitate this whole process and to eliminate, if possible, the possibility of providing opportunities for parents expecting their first child, to gain even a day's experience in learning parenting skills. Babies after delivery (unless they are being breast-fed) could go directly from the delivery room to the arms of the skilled parents waiting at the delivery room door with a court order granting them temporary legal custody of the child just delivered. A millionaire would certainly be in a position to try to obtain legal custody of at least 37 children provided one of the millionaire's goals is to start a children's group home.

Let's conclude by assuming that after Dr. Eve Keys's expert testimony in court, she begins assuming child care responsibilities for her grandson after the sudden and tragic death of her son and daughter-in-law occurring the day after the hearing regarding Faith. This sounds like a plan based on sound judgment *until* a couple who have earned the recognition for obtaining the highest scores on record in a battery of psychological tests—file for legal custody of Dr. Keys's grandson by virtue of their superior parenting skills, maturity, emotional stability, and insight. Will it take an experience such as that of Dr. Keys losing legal custody of a grandchild to stress the importance and tragedy of totally disregarding the constitutional rights of a parent-child relationship? Let's hope people and, in particular, expert witnesses with a perspective of Dr. Keys's perception of a child's best interests will wake up before it is too late.

Interestingly enough, the judge in this example is the son of an alcoholic mother and a father with a history of marital problems. The well-respected judge grew up in the home of his parents and, considering the problems of his home environment, he may have achieved a goal quite different from becoming a judge if another family had filed for custody of him.

Again I ask, in considering the best interests of a child, let's not have the "tunnel vision" of just Dr. Keys's perspective unless you are working toward a world in which the completion of psychological testing and custody evaluations would be mandatory for all expectant parents to determine if their child has the right to be raised in their homes. *The choice is up to you.* I suggest you make the choice wisely and give it the serious consideration and thought it warrants because the decision made has serious implications for all children, parents, and potential parents in the future. Children like Faith have to depend on the sound judgment of those persons who will make decisions based on a *fair, objective assessment* of *all* factors involved in a custody case. Let's hope that you are not one of the persons who has to learn "the hard way" about the implications of a decision like that of Dr. Eve Keys. *The choice is yours!*

Chapter 21

ADDITIONAL RELEVANT CUSTODY ISSUES

The custody area is complex and requires ongoing research and experience. Any specialized area contains its own unique set of issues which usually always results in diversity of opinions among lay persons as well as professionals who have expertise in this specialized area. This chapter deals with some of the relevant issues confronting professionals who are actively involved in custody cases. The issues that will be discussed include the following: (1) physical and sexual abuse allegations in custody cases; (2) the issue of lifestyle; (3) visitation conflicts; and, (4) grandparents or other non-parents versus parents. The importance of viewing each case with a focus on the particular combination of factors unique to that particular custody case rather than utilizing generalizations in viewing cases during the evaluation or investigation procedure, is important to consider at all times.

The issues covered in this chapter are considered important issues that deserve serious consideration of not only each issue discussed, but of the implications or the manner in which each issue is dealt with by judges, attorneys, mental health professionals, and by the Appellate Court as well as the Supreme Court. Critical decisions in some of the areas discussed in this chapter have very critical and relevant implications not only for now but for the future. The issues selected to be discussed are especially meaningful due to this author's direct involvement in custody cases that required formulation of facts and opinions directly related to each issue. It is an impossibility to discuss every important issue in the custody area in any one book or manual, let alone in one chapter, but it is my hope that the issues presented will spark interest among professionals as well as among litigants in custody cases, to become actively involved in trying to insure that the current laws are in the best interests of children and that other laws do not violate basic constitutional rights. If laws need to be clarified or revised in some areas, helping to educate others regarding this need and their being actively involved in efforts to bring about necessary or needed changes in the law, would be a desired goal or outcome of this chapter.

A.
PHYSICAL AND SEXUAL ABUSE ALLEGATIONS
IN CUSTODY CASES

There seems to be an increasing number of suspected physical and sexual abuse allegations that become an important consideration in determining the best interests of children in custody cases. An allegation of suspected physical or sexual abuse of children by a custodial or non-custodial parent is obviously extremely serious, particularly if the allegation is true. But it also warrants a thorough, conscientious investigation due to the fact that if a parent knowingly makes a serious abuse allegation involving the other parent either without any factual basis or without facts or observations to form a basis for reasonable suspicion, then the results can be devastating for the alleged victim and perpetrator as well. There are instances in which serious allegations have been made up by a parent or a child encouraged to give false information to professionals mandated by law to report suspected child abuse or neglect to the Illinois Department of Children and Family Services in hopes that the end result will be the parent making the allegation to be awarded permanent legal custody of the child or children involved in the contested custody litigation.

An allegation of physical and/or sexual abuse can be the result of any of the following possibilities: (1) a parent may have genuine concern regarding the possibility that a son or daughter may have been abused as the result of comments made by the child and/or observations of unexplained injuries to the child or injuries in which the alleged perpetrator's explanation for the child's injury is inconsistent with the nature of the injury (for example, an explanation that a child was hurt while playing ball but there are observable injuries resembling numerous cigarette burns on the child's arms, legs and back, (2) a parent may be so determined to obtain legal custody of the children that the parent will make up allegations involving the other parent or will encourage the child to make comments to others that based on comments a child makes, a professional may conclude there is basis to suspect that the child has been abused by one of the parents or, (3) a child may have a strong preference for the mother and due to a concern that the father may be granted custody, may decide to allege that he or she was physically or sexually abused by the father. The child in this instance may not realize the seriousness of such allegations or the implications of the abuse investigation that in all probability will begin soon after the allegation is brought to the attention of any professional who is mandated to report suspected neglect or abuse of children, as is the case in Illinois.

A further complication is the fact that it is often extremely difficult to determine if the abuse actually occurred. In the majority of alleged sexual abuse cases, it is typical to have the child's version of the alleged abuse countered by the alleged perpetrator's denial of the truth of the allegation. In most sexual abuse cases as well as in many cases of physical abuse of children, there are no witnesses that could be interviewed in order to help determine the truth of the allegation. Many types of sexual abuse can occur without any medical evidence being possible. Many injuries to children are not the result of physical abuse but are injuries resulting from accidents. If a child is not old enough to be a credible witness, it becomes even more difficult to determine the cause of injuries to children.

If there are facts to indicate abuse has occurred, it is important to determine the seriousness of the allegation, the frequency of abusive incidents, the age of the child who has been abused, and the contributing factors that helped lead to the abuse taking place. It is also important to consider the perpetrator's attitude toward the abuse incident, the parent's willingness to correct the conditions that are the basis for the abuse and the motivation for the parent's wanting to learn healthy ways to deal with emotions such as anger, depression, or frustration. The abuse incident should also be viewed in the context of all other factors relating to the perpetrator's situation as well as the factors relating to the other parent's situation.

For example, one parent may physically abuse a child on one occasion resulting in a small bruise on the child's buttock area. Investigation of that same parent reveals a loving parent who is quite capable of assuming parental responsibilities for the child, the parent who has been the primary one who has assumed responsibility for child care tasks since the child's birth, and the parent has no history of abusive or neglectful behavior or of exhibiting any emotional problems. The non-abusive parent may be an alcoholic and/or drug addict with poor prognosis for recovering from the addiction. If the parent's drug or alcohol addiction interferes significantly with the litigant's parenting abilities (both quantity of time the parent spends with the child in addition to the quality of parenting), then the abusive parent may be the least detrimental alternative when considering the best long-range plan for the child.

Abuse allegations should always be taken seriously because if there are no facts to substantiate the allegation, it is certainly important to try to determine if one of the litigants made the allegation without any factual basis or if the litigant believes that the other parent is abusive and considers the abuse to be a reality even in view of an extensive investigation resulting in no facts to substantiate the abuse. A child may also be denying the truth of the allegation but the one parent persists in communicating to the child (both verbally and/or non-verbally) that the alleged abuse is true.

In closing, it cannot be stressed enough that any abuse or neglect allegations must be viewed within the context of the validity of the allegation as well as viewing all factors involved in the child's situation in each litigant's home. It is not just one fact that determines the best interests of a child. It is a combination of facts considering the child's individual needs, the parenting abilities of each litigant, and each litigant and child in relation to the environmental factors involved.

B.
WHEN CUSTODY LITIGATION INVOLVES PARENT VERSUS GRANDPARENT

When a contested custody case involves a natural or adoptive parent as one litigant and a grandparent or other relative of the child as the other litigant, the case becomes more complicated in some ways because it is extremely serious when one realizes that if a grandparent legally obtains permanent legal custody of a child, then a precedent is set with very serious implications for the future. For example, a case in which a grandparent obtains permanent legal custody of a grandchild can result in the future in numerous contested custody cases being initiated in court between a natural parent or parents and grandparents or other relatives of the child. Due to the serious implications, lets focus on the reason for and *the necessity of a parent's right to legally be given priority over other person's rights to obtain permanent legal custody of a child.*

First, consider the following assumptions or beliefs that seem to have a factual basis: (1) as a general rule, most grade schools, high schools or universities throughout the country do not offer any classes in parenting;

a student's successfully completing a class in parenting is not a mandatory requirement for graduation of any type; (2) many people know basically the child care practices of their own parents which would include child care practices that might be abusive, neglectful and/or certainly not the practices that would be advocated by child care experts; (3) many parents find that when their first child is born, they are relying on instinct, speculation and trial and error methods of child rearing; they try one method or idea and if it does not seem to work successfully, then they will begin experimenting on other approaches hoping to find a method that will bring about the desired behavior in the child; (4) throughout generations, many parents repeat the same neglectful or abusive child rearing practices they learned from their parents; (5) most teenagers and parents in their early 20's are not as mature, skilled, experienced, or knowledgeable about parenting skills as older parents, including grandparents, nor should they be expected to be. After all, most people growing up will at times exhibit behavior which is immature, self-defeating, negative, and which would not be the result of good judgment. Fortunately, most people can learn from mistakes, experience and by obtaining increased knowledge. For example, many respected and skilled alcohol counselors may be alcoholics themselves who successfully learned attitudes or ideas and practice daily behavior that helps them maintain sobriety; (6) the majority of parents have a desire to learn to be the best parents they are capable of becoming; (7) the majority of parents love their children and do not intentionally want to do anything that would affect a child adversely.

One of the basic rights a child has is the right to be able to be raised in the home of a parent or parents, provided the parent is willing to assume child care responsibilities. Even in cases where a parent has severely abused or neglected a child, it is legally very difficult to terminate parental rights. Most children who are in foster care placement temporarily are eventually returned to the home of a parent by courts and Department of Children and Family Services staff. One major goal of Department of Children and Family Services is protection of children, but a secondary goal would be the strengthening of the family unit and to attempt to keep families together if at all possible, unless there are facts to substantiate that a child will be in danger of being abused, neglected or in some other danger by remaining in the home of a parent.

Many families have definite financial limitations and some families live at almost a poverty level financially. Many homes which do not offer material advantages may still offer a loving and nurturing environment in which a child feels secure, loved and important. The song "Coat of Many Colors" sung by Dolly Parton reflects her childhood of poverty, but yet one that was full of love from her family. The "Coat of Many Colors" Dolly wore to school was handmade by her mother and, as Dolly describes it, love was sewn into every stitch. By contrast, there are parents who offer numerous material advantages to children but leave out the most important advantages of love, understanding, and taking time to talk to and spend time with their children. It is probably very fortunate that there are some things that money just cannot buy.

If a judge awards permanent legal custody of a child to a grandparent when a parent is wanting the responsibility of raising the child and particularly if there are no facts to substantiate that the child has been abused or neglected in the home of the parent, then the child may grow up with many questions regarding why he or she can't live with a parent. The child may begin resenting the grandparent for depriving him of the opportunity to live with a parent like the majority of children are able to do.

In retrospect, just remember that many grandparents today might have been in a position of not having the opportunity to gain knowledge, experience, and skills in parenting if at a time when the grandparent went through a stage of not being very mature, a court order took legal custody of the child away from the grandparent. It is realistically difficult to learn parenting skills if one has no opportunity to be a parent or parent substitute.

The legal rights of parents being given priority over grandparent's rights to custody of a child has a sound theoretical basis as hopefully has been illustrated. Parent's rights to custody of their child, and children's rights to be raised by a parent, should be viewed very seriously because it is a valuable right and privilege that should not be taken away without good reasons based on *facts* and *not speculation, even if the speculation is by an expert witness such as a Ph.D., psychologist or psychiatrist.*

Just as with any profession, no professional can be 100% accurate in their area of expertise. It is also very true that some professionals are more competent or skilled than others. One professional may be quick to accept as fact an allegation of medical neglect without talking to a physician about the case, whereas another professional with the same information presented would not draw any conclusions without more information, and information from a physician is *essential* to determine the validity of any medical neglect allegation. A professional without

Figure 4. One of the best presents a child in a custody case could ever receive is for both parents to cooperate in helping the child to have a loving positive relationship with each parent. Children have a right to each parent being active participants in the life of the child. After all, one of the most valuable gifts a parent can ever give a child is his or her time.

expertise in the medical area could no more reach a conclusion on a medical neglect allegation than a physician could administer a battery of psychological tests to a person without any expertise in that area. It is essential that each professional not only stay within their realm of expertise but also utilize and consult with the expertise of other professionals when it is needed. *Each profession has much to contribute but can also contribute even more by benefiting from not only the expertise of its own profession, but also from the expertise of other professions.*

Natural and adoptive parents, but most importantly children, have their whole future at stake. Realize the implications of not recognizing the rights of children to have daily relationships (parent-child relationships) and to have the opportunity to grow up in the home of a parent or parents.

C.
VISITATION ISSUES

There are routinely court orders sent to the Department of Children and Family Services ordering that an investigation be completed focusing on visitation issues only. Those particular issues may include any of the following: (1) a parent wanting to decrease the frequency of the non-custodial parent's visitation with the child; (2) a non-custodial parent requesting increased visitation with a child; (3) a parent requesting that the non-custodial parent's visitation be supervised or limited due to concerns evolving around a custodial parent's questioning the suitability of a non-custodial parent's home for unsupervised visitation with the child or questioning the non-custodial parent's ability to provide adequate care and supervision to children during unsupervised visitation. For example, a non-custodial parent's excessive alcohol and/or drug use (in the past or currently), a pattern of criminal behavior such as violent behavior, or a non-custodial parent's lack of parenting skills and/or experience may contribute to legitimate concerns over the safety and well-being of a child during visitations.

Certainly in most instances, it is beneficial for a child to have as active an involvement from both parents in his life as possible. A child usually benefits from both parents taking an active role in child rearing even after a divorce. But at the same time, a child needs to be in a safe environment during periods of visitation and should not be put in a position where he may be injured.

Visitation issues can be investigated in much the same process as investigations related to custody issues. Methods can be utilized (questions and observations) which would help to assess: (1) problems or concerns regarding visitation; (2) child's reaction to the visitation if child is old enough to interview; (3) observation of the non-custodial parent with the child; (4) trying to obtain any facts or observations that would substantiate the validity and/or relevancy of expressed concerns or conflicts regarding visitation.

If a concern is expressed centering around the safety issues related to the non-custodial parent's house, *it is essential that a home visit be made* to assess whether or not the non-custodial parent's home offers a safe home environment for visits. It is also important to consider the age of the child, frequency of visitation, duration of visits, and other relevant factors helpful in the assessment process. *During any custody investigation, it is sometimes beneficial to take pictures during the course of the investigation which can include pictures of the home environment or pictures representing interactions of a child with litigants.*

It should also be stressed that a typical visitation schedule for a child and a non-custodial parent that might be included routinely in a court order would be for a non-custodial parent to visit a child every other weekend and every other holiday, and one or two blocks of time during the summer, without any consideration of factors such as the following: (1) the child's age; (2) the child's and parent's interactions with each other; (3) the parent's ability to adequately meet the physical, emotional, medical, educational and spiritual needs of the child during visitation; (4) whether the home environment utilized for visitations is safe (particularly for infants or pre-school age children); (5) the feelings of the child regarding the frequency or length of visitations (particularly if the child is a teenager); (6) an assessment of whether or not the parent has a problem (such as with drugs, alcohol or an emotional problem) that might have a detrimental effect on the child or might result in a child being abused or neglected during a visit; or, (7) whether or not a parent's spouse, live-in boyfriend or girlfriend, or other person that would be part of the visiting environment would have a detrimental effect on the child.

Visitations should be set up for the benefit of the child. Depending on the assessment, it may be advisable to restrict visitation or even terminate visits if facts are present to indicate that scheduled visitation could result in a child being in potential risk of harm or being affected adversely by visitations.

Visitation schedules should take into consideration a child's age and developmental needs. *Dianne Skafte is co-author of a published article that very clearly contributes valuable insights in regard to this entire area.*

It would seem that typical court testimony (not involving a professional who has thoroughly investigated or evaluated the essential factors in regard to each litigant) might easily result in court decisions that could place children in environments that would not be nurturing for children, but instead would be detrimental to their well-being. Judges do not have "crystal balls" to be able to foresee the future. It is easy for a person to be critical of a judge's decision in a custody case, but *it is not fair or realistic to expect a judge to make decisions that take into consideration critical information if it is not available for his review at the court hearing.*

With the current concern about AIDS, it would be a realistic expectation that all custody decisions concerning children of parents who have been diagnosed as having AIDS will be particularly critical to all those individuals who are affected by those decisions. For the sake of the children involved, lets hope judges have access to as much vital information as possible prior to making critical decisions since court decisions can be based only on information available to the court. Professionals who specialize in the custody area could potentially become an invaluable aid to children and courts, as long as laws provide this option.

In summary, there will always be cases in which a decision regarding visitation could be as critical to a child as a decision regarding which parent will have permanent legal custody of the child. It would not be unusual for the average lay person or even the average professional to *not* recognize the value of professionals who have a dedication, commitment and "burning desire" to provide quality services to children in the custody area. For the sake of the innocent victims of contested custody litigation, let's hope that there will never come a time when legislators, attorneys and judges will *not* recognize the value of a professional investigation and/or evaluation by a professional with expertise in the custody area.

D.
ISSUES RELATING TO LIFESTYLES

It is easy at times for a naive examiner or investigator to place major importance on minor criteria such as lifestyle and even permit a person's lifestyle to be considered more relevant than major criteria such as the criteria of psychological parent or a litigant's flexibility regarding visitation in custody recommendations.

Many persons would conclude that if the choice is between a happily married couple offering a middle or upper class home environment versus a parent with a live-in boyfriend or girlfriend (with no legal commitment between the two adults) and a lower socioeconomic background, the more desirable choice would be the married couple. This may be the choice that would be in the best interests of the child but there is just as much possibility that the choice would not be the best suited to meet the needs of the children. What is more important than the fact of the non-married adults living together is the child's relationship not only to the parent but to the parent substitute. In some instances, it is possible for a child to be closer emotionally to a parent substitute than a step-parent or even a parent. It would be particularly significant if the parent substitute was active in helping with child care responsibilities, spent time in educational and recreational activities with the child, and other similar factors.

We should be cognizant of the fact that natural, adoptive and step-parents can be physically abusive, sexually abusive and neglectful of children just as readily as a live-in boyfriend or girlfriend of a parent. The above example merely illustrates the importance of looking at the entire picture when reviewing a situation and not placing major significance on a factor that using your own value system may be immoral, unacceptable and not in good judgment, unless there are facts to substantiate your opinion. Certainly, it would not be advocated by most people that there be a dictatorship that allows no freedom of choice regarding lifestyle, values, religion, and other factors. Unless a lifestyle is detrimental to others in some way and/or adversely affects a child, it should not be given primary consideration.

In one of my custody investigations, a parent's home was so inflexible and strict in regard to expected behaviors of the children that the children were not allowed to develop their own personalities and potential. The children could not express their ideas, be involved in discussions concerning their feelings and they also had total lack of privacy to the extent their rooms were routinely searched, private letters read by the parent, and phone conversations taped. In this instance, the lifestyle had an adverse effect on the children and some of the major criteria may be less important than the lifestyle issue in this particular case.

In summary, each criteria needs to be assessed, not only in regard to the absence, presence or extent of being present in each litigant's home, but the effect each criteria has on each child physically, emotionally, educationally, medically or spiritually.

E.
INTERVIEWING PROCESS

The interviewing process is an essential part of any custody investigation or evaluation. The questions need to be designed to attempt to provide information relevant to the major and minor criteria considered in determining which litigant can provide the best permanent home for the children (considering the best interests of the children). It is essential to interview children over five years of age at school if at all possible or in another neutral setting such as the office or a restaurant such as Hardee's. It is better to interview children individually on the same day to try to minimize the children's being influenced or pressured by litigants or children having an opportunity to discuss the questions with each other prior to completing an interview with the social worker. By interviewing children the same day (one interview immediately following another interview), there would not be an opportunity for children to discuss questions asked until after the initial interview.

It is best to ask open ended questions to provide opportunities for children or adults to volunteer information that is considered the most relevant. It is helpful to ask specific questions that would help to assess the truth of any allegations. It is important that litigants and children understand the purpose of the interviews and that they try to include all information related directly to parenting abilities. It is important that questions asked of children be worded in language that can be understood by a child the age of the child being interviewed. If an answer seems vague or unclear, be sure to ask additional questions that would help to clarify the information.

Since everyone has different perceptions or views of events, it is important to understand the collateral's, litigant's, or child's point of view. For example, if a collateral relates that Litigant A is an alcoholic, do not just accept this conclusion as a fact but ask more specific questions such as: Why do you believe Litigant A is an alcoholic? Have you ever observed Litigant A drinking alcoholic beverages? If so, questions relating to the frequency, circumstances, and the extent of drinking on each occasion (number of drinks in addition to over what period of time each observation was made) should be some of the questions asked.

During the interview, it is important to try to keep in control of the interview. There are some individuals who may ignore or disregard the question asked and try to elaborate at length on events that happened years ago. Unless information has a direct bearing on the parenting abilities of litigants or has a direct effect on the children, it may be information that is not needed or relevant.

In summary, ask relevant open-ended questions designed to elicit information that will help in assessing or evaluating criteria that would pertain to each litigant's home.

Figure 5. Children in custody cases usually feel an emotional pull by each parent and feel under pressure not only to choose one parent over the other, but also to make this preference known to others, including the other parent.

F.

THE COMPLEXITIES OF CUSTODY INVESTIGATIONS

Professionals who are involved in completing custody investigations or evaluations will in all probability agree that the majority of contested child custody cases are quite difficult and complex. A professional or lay person who has not been involved in custody cases will probably not have the appreciation for or comprehension of the challenges inherent in the custody area. *It is usually only after a person has completed extensive research and gained extensive first-hand experience in this specialized area that a knowledge base is present upon which on-going research and experience can strengthen a professional's expertise and understanding in this area.*

In order for any professional to perform a thorough investigation or evaluation, one first has to have the specialized knowledge and skills essential. Some of the skills utilized include investigative, interviewing and assessment skills. Do not be naive enough to believe that any professional with a Ph.D. in psychology or psychiatry automatically is an expert in the custody area just because the Ph.D. entitles the professional to be considered an "expert witness" in court.

In my experience in the custody area, I have encountered psychologists (such as Dr. Gordon Plumb) who obviously have expertise in the custody area and who are in reality "true experts" due to specialized research and experience in the custody area in addition to having completed the educational requirements of Ph.D. Psychologists such as Dr. Plumb complete thorough evaluations based on interviews with *all litigants and children involved in a custody case,* interview collaterals, and complete appropriate testing. Dr. Plumb will not become involved in a custody evaluation unless he is able to see all litigants and children involved in each particular custody case. *It is my contention that a "true expert in the custody area" would refuse to take an adversarial position and recommend one of the litigants for custody unless the psychologist evaluated each litigant himself.*

In contrast are psychologists who may have a Ph.D., but who have very little expertise in the custody area as well as having virtually not read the first book or article written by experts in the custody area. A psychologist (even with a Ph.D.) with little or no expertise in the custody area would in all probability not be hesitant to take adversarial positions in custody cases. This type of psychologist or other mental health professional would even be willing (as long as his or her fee is paid by one of the litigants) to testify in court as an advocate for one of the litigants in the custody recommendation, without even having met the other litigant until the day of court. In this case, the "expert witness" is being negligent, unprofessional, and should be considered "dangerous," especially if judges don't recognize the "hired gun" approach of the psychologist.

Let us consider at least some of the complexities encountered in the majority of investigations or evaluations. One difficulty is that in custody cases, the professional has the awesome task of trying to arrive at the closest proximity to the truth in several important areas affecting a child from birth to the date of the custody investigation. An investigation of alleged abuse or neglect often involves determining the truth of an allegation that may involve one incident in a child's life in contrast to a custody investigation that may include from two months to eight years to fourteen years of a child's life—including sometimes several allegations of abuse or neglect, as is often the case in the custody area.

Let's further consider the following statements which seem to be true, based on research and experience in custody cases:

1. Children usually love both parents and do not want to alienate either parent.
2. Children usually experience loyalty conflicts during pending custody litigation.
3. Children usually will tend to tell each parent (or parent's attorney) what the child perceives that each particular parent wants the child to say; therefore, the child may in actuality be making contradictory statements, depending on whom he is talking to.
4. Litigants usually always relate allegations about a spouse or ex-spouse. Many times an allegation is true, but it also happens often that an allegation may be exaggerated or may even be a complete fabrication.
5. Litigants perceive experiences differently and usually a professional hears two contradictory versions of each allegation. Even two witnesses to an accident will, many times, relate totally different versions of the "facts."
6. A custody case is usually always full of strong emotions on the part of the litigants and children. Anger, resentment, jealousy, depression and/or love are emotions that can easily distort the reality of situations. Time also has a way of distorting reality. Collaterals usually provide contradictory versions of allegations.
7. Contested custody cases tend to focus on the negatives or weaknesses of each litigant rather than on a focus of strengths.

In summary, thorough investigations or evaluations must include an assessment that is based on a thorough analysis of all the data obtained during the investigation. It is indeed a rare opportunity to encounter a custody case that is "clear-cut" or "simple." Custody cases are usually complex, challenging, and thus require that investigations be completed by professionals who have expertise in the custody area based on specialized knowledge and skills. Only then will justice to children (involved in the middle of a contested custody litigation) be a part of contested custody litigation.

G.
SUGGESTIONS FOR THE FUTURE

It seems that courts, litigants and children involved in contested custody cases could all benefit by the following procedures which might be able to be introduced in the future in a bill that, if passed, may become additions to the current Illinois Marriage and Dissolution of Marriage Act.

1. An attorney is appointed to represent the children and be in the position to insure that the best interests of the children are considered during all phases of the court process.

2. There be specific time limitations in the court process so that a temporary custody order does not result in an order for permanent custody primarily due to the continuity of relationships resulting from a year or more delay in the scheduled court hearings. A person having temporary custody may provide adequate care of children on a temporary basis, but yet not be the parent or litigant who can provide the best quality of parenting on a permanent basis. It is better for children in general if they don't have to be in a situation over a prolonged period of time in which in all probability they experience loyalty conflicts. A long drawn-out contested custody case contributes to the litigants and children experiencing anger, frustration and animosity.

3. Ideally, more than one mental health professional such as a psychologist and a social worker (preferably a certified social worker and/or an MSW) should both be involved in completing independent evaluations and investigations. Both professionals could work together with the litigants and attorneys to try to explore the possibility of the case being settled out of court. Hopefully, the evaluation and investigation will complement each other with the goal of resolving the matter without an adversarial proceeding.

4. It should be mandatory that all contested custody proceedings include an objective, thorough evaluation and/or assessment and investigation of parenting abilities conducted by a qualified professional evaluator

or investigator with a theoretical knowledge base in the complexities inherent in the contested custody case. Without such an assessment, a litigant who has the most knowledgeable and skilled attorney or the litigant who makes the most favorable impression (such as an articulate person or a person with more prestige or influence) may obtain legal custody of a child, but yet be the parent who has not assumed the major child care responsibilities for the child and is not the psychological parent for the child or children involved.

5. Parenting classes should be a mandatory requirement in all high school and college curriculum for all students prior to a student's receiving a high school diploma or graduating from college. The majority of high school students eventually become parents or parent substitutes without having been afforded the opportunity to learn parenting skills needed to prepare for assuming parental responsibilities.

6. All attorneys, litigants and judges involved in contested custody cases all have a right to request (by court order) involvement of Department of Children and Family Services social workers and/or psychologists, or other mental health professionals to conduct an objective custody investigation and/or evaluation.

7. It should be mandatory that all professionals involved in custody cases need to receive specialized training in the specialized area of custody covering the major custody issues. Minimum criteria need to be determined in this regard. Videotape and tape recorders should be an option that can be utilized by professionals during the completion of a custody evaluation or investigation provided the litigants and/or judge approve of this particular plan.

8. There needs to be more follow up and research involving custody cases settled out of court as well as after a court hearing with a goal of evaluating the success of the prior court decision regarding child custody.

9. There should be the provision of judges having legal authority to appoint an attorney to represent a litigant who has facts to document an inability financially to afford an attorney. This is to help minimize the opportunity for a court decision to result from a decision influenced primarily from the expertise of an attorney and his courtroom tactics instead of being based on consideration of criteria listed as relevant in determining parenting abilities. There should also be a provision for a litigant to appeal a custody decision even if the litigant cannot financially afford an attorney and cannot be represented by legal aid services for reasons such as lack of funding.

10. If approved by the judge, a stipulation can be recommended that a custody decision is intended to be a final decision but can be set up so it would be subject to court review in a year. Requiring an updated evaluation or assessment by qualified professionals could be a part of the court-ordered stipulation so that the expertise of an objective professional would be available to all parties to the custody proceeding prior to the final court review of the case.

11. If the litigants to any custody proceeding live within a seventy-five mile radius from the professional completing the custody evaluation or investigation, it should be legally mandatory that the same professional be court-ordered to see all parties to the custody proceedings so that not more than one psychologist, social worker or mental health professional from each specialized profession is involved in the same custody case.

12. If court orders are consistently violated by one or more litigants, there needs to be a realistic system worked out to bring the case back for court review without a litigant being required to pay an attorney a substantial amount of money before the case is brought to the court's attention. Most violations of court orders are detrimental to children.

13. All custody investigations and evaluations need to be conducted by qualified professionals who possess the specialized knowledge, skills and expertise essential to be able to utilize the methods successfully. All professionals in the custody area need to be involved in on-going evaluations of the methods utilized. All professionals in the specialized area should also be required to meet at least the following minimum criteria before utilizing methods outlined in this book: (1) preferably an MSW, CSW, ACSW Social Worker or MA Counselor or other mental health professional with specialized training in the relevant issues that are a part of all custody evaluations or investigations. The custody area needs to be a specialized area that has its own knowledge-base.

Laws need to be set up (if not already a reality) so that there is a legal provision in each state to involve professionals in conducting custody investigations or evaluations. This needs to be available to all litigants and children, regardless of their financial ability to afford professional services. In this author's experience, many litigants are not even in a financial position to afford an attorney, let alone other professionals. Many litigants borrow money in order to pay an attorney's fee and may be $3,000 to $4,000 in debt for attorney's fees alone before the custody proceeding is legally resolved. It is this author's firm belief that children should not be denied professional services that are designed to benefit them due to a litigant's inability to pay for services. Possibly legislators could address this issue and seek a feasible solution that could be legally implemented.

This author has a firm belief in the need for professional specialization within state agencies (such as the Department of Children and Family Services) to provide court-ordered custody investigations. It is not logical that a child welfare specialist, just be virtue of being employed in that position, *automatically* will possess specialized knowledge, skill and expertise in the custody area any more than a parent would automatically possess parenting skills just be virtue of legally being a parent. Expertise in a specialized area is not magically bestowed upon a child welfare specialist the second he or she is employed in that position. True expertise in an area is the result of experience, knowledge, skill, motivation, genuine interest and ability to demonstrate that expertise and is *not* the automatic end result of possessing a title such as "child welfare specialist." If you don't believe this, just be sure to notify me if you are ever in a situation where you need surgery because arrangements can easily be made for a friend of mine who has the title, "Doc," to perform your surgery. With your philosophy, it should not even bother you in the least that the person who will perform your surgery is an actress who is quite clumsy, has narcolepsy, gets sick and vomits at the sight of blood, and sneezes often. Hopefully, the picture is quite clear.

Problems relating to individual litigants or the home environments of litigants in this author's experience have included the following: Abusive parents, neglectful parents, verbal abuse, violence, criminal records, alcohol or drug problems, emotional problems to the extreme that one mother was looking in the neighborhood for her child when, in fact, the child was in the mother's home, and a parent having a history of living in the streets for over a year. Several custody investigations in which I have been involved have also had an investigation of alleged child abuse or neglect being conducted at the same time as my custody investigation. Some investigations have resulted in indicated reports, meaning factual evidence to substantiate that the child was abused or neglected.

Many children in a custody situation may not actually be physically or sexually abused or neglected; however, the emotional pressure children in contested custody typically feel is certainly detrimental to their emotional well-being and may even result in the child becoming neurotic, psychotic, or even taking drastic measures such as commiting suicide.

The emotional welfare of a child is just as important as the physical well-being of a child.

Children in the midst of contested custody litigation have the right to professional intervention enabling them to legally live in the environment that will be the most nurturing emotionally and that will be an environment in which abuse, neglect or other detrimental behavior would be the least likely to occur.

Figure 6. If both parents in a contested custody proceedings would focus on the needs of the child, it would help the child feel like a king. A child should be showered with love and positive attention by both parents to the extent he or she feels very worthwhile instead of feeling like a pawn on a chessboard.

Chapter 22

CHILDREN'S RIGHTS IN CUSTODY CASES

During this author's specialization in conducting court-ordered custody investigations as well as providing testimony during numerous custody hearings, several ideas seem to surface as being the most important needs or rights of all children who are in the middle of contested custody cases. These rights can be summarized as seventeen rights of all children in contested custody cases. Most of the rights have direct implications for litigants. After reviewing the list of rights, the implications in terms of expectations of the type of attitude and behavior litigants should ideally exhibit, will be quite obvious. It is beneficial to keep these ideas in mind in assessing parenting abilities of litigants as well as the major criteria each litigant offers.

SEVENTEEN RIGHTS OF ALL CHILDREN IN CUSTODY CASES

1. Each child has right to hear only positive comments about his mother from his father and only positive comments about his father from his mother.

2. Each child has a right to not have to lose either parent. In other words, each child needs both parents, for those are the only parents the child has.

3. Each child has a right to visit the non-custodial parent. Even in cases in which a child has been abused by a non-custodial parent, visits can be restricted, supervised and arranged to ensure the safety of the child.

4. Each child has a right to encouragement from his own father to have a positive loving relationship with his mother and to encouragement from his mother to have a positive loving relationship with his father.

5. Each child has a right to live with a parent as long as the parent is able and willing to assume parental responsibilities and the child is not abused, neglected or at risk of harm in the parent's home.

6. Each child has a right not to feel guilty about custody conflicts, as the child is *not* responsible for the conflicts and is the innocent victim in the situation.

7. Each child has a right to receive unconditional love and positive regard from each parent, regardless of which parent the child would prefer to live with.

8. Each child has a right to *not* be included in any conflicts or disagreements between the parents.

9. Each child has a right to both parents being active participants in the life of the child.

10. Each child has a right to *not* feel pressured emotionally by his parents or other relatives.

11. Each child has a right to a parent's intervention in the event the child is subjected to comments of a negative nature about either parent. A parent can politely tell a person making negative comments that it is not appropriate to discuss negative information about the parent in front of the child.

12. Each child has a right to legislation that provides legal mandates for professional intervention in custody cases such as investigations and/or evaluations being provided by professionals with expertise in the custody area. *Professionals providing services in the custody area need specialized knowledge and experience in the complexities of contested custody.*

13. Each child has a right to professional services from agency staff (such as from the Illinois Department of Children and Family Services) regardless of whether or not his parents are financially able and/or willing to pay for the professional services.

14. Each child has a right to have each parent abide by existing court orders and to *not* intentionally violate any orders.

15. Each child has a right to professional services from social workers or other mental health professionals who recognize the importance and significance of such professional intervention and who can demonstrate skill and expertise in the custody area. A child's future is at stake and it deserves quality services from caring concerned professionals.

16. Each child has a right to actually *be* a child who would *not* be expected to be concerned with adult problems. A child should be able to be involved in recreational and educational activities typical of a child his age.

17. Each child has a right to expect each parent to work cooperatively together in focusing on the child's needs and feelings as being the most

important consideration in all decisions each parent makes. Each parent's attitude and behavior should demonstrate an understanding and focus on the needs of the child.

If the above seventeen rights were completely understood and followed by litigants in contested custody cases, it is certain that there would be more cases settled out of court with assistance from professionals. There would be a minimum of hostility, resentment and anger exhibited between litigants. As a result, children would have less emotional problems. Litigants also, in all probability, would exhibit much less neurotic or psychotic behavior that might otherwise be the end result of custody conflicts encouraged by the current adversarial system.

Each professional involved in providing services to children and courts in custody cases needs to consider the above children's rights as being like a blueprint from which a custody investigation is designed. It is essential that the primary focus of such investigation is the child and his needs and feelings. *The child's best interests should always be paramount.*

Figure 7. Wouldn't it be wonderful if children involved in contested custody proceedings could just relax, enjoy being a child, and not have to feel under such pressure emotionally?

Chapter 23

CHILDREN HAVE A RIGHT TO COURT-ORDERED CUSTODY INVESTIGATIONS

The innocent victims of contested custody cases are the children who are caught in the middle of the court litigation. Children depend on the existing laws, courts, and professionals to provide services that will result in decisions that will be beneficial to them and in their best interests. After all, the children have their entire future at stake and the custody decision is bound to have a profound effect on their future.

In order to illustrate why objective investigations or evaluations are essential in providing an invaluable aid to the court in custody decisions, let's consider the following hypothetical cases. Listed are brief descriptions of seventeen litigants who are trying to obtain permanent legal custody of children.

1. One litigant is a diagnosed alcoholic who still engages in periodic "drinking binges."
2. Another litigant is diagnosed as a drug addict who still is tempted to take non-prescription illegal drugs.
3. Another litigant has a history of living in the streets for over a year. He sleeps in a car or truck or on a park bench year-round, may or may not eat a meal during the day, and takes a bath at friends' houses if permitted.
4. A litigant has a history of exhibiting violent behavior resulting in injuries to a spouse and/or child.
5. A litigant's home environment contains safety hazards, particularly for pre-school age children such as broken glass in the yard, knives within reach of a toddler, guns accessible to a child, tools in the yard, cabinets not child-proof, large holes in the floor, a wood-burning heating stove within reach of toddlers, and medicine lying around the house within reach of a child.
6. A litigant has abused a child in the past (physical or sexual abuse) or has a definite potential for abusing children.
7. A litigant has neglected a child in the past or has a definite potential to neglect children.

8. A litigant drives a car (with children as passengers) while under the influence of alcoholic beverages and/or drugs.
9. A litigant has a history of emotional problems to the extent he or she on occasions looks for a child at times the child is inside the litigant's house.
10. A litigant permits children under age 18 to drink alcoholic beverages and/or smoke marijuana.
11. A litigant has left an infant asleep in a crib alone and unsupervised while she goes to visit a friend for a few hours, thinking that the baby will be asleep until she returns home.
12. A litigant expects the child to "spy" on the other parent and report every activity of the parent.
13. A litigant has a combination of the above problems.
14. A litigant tries to place pressure emotionally on the child in regard to the custody situation.
15. A litigant is clearly self-centered and does not focus on the needs of children.
16. A litigant is not really wanting child care responsibilities and has no intention of providing care for the child himself if he gets custody. He plans to let a couple in their seventies assume full responsibility for the child on a daily basis while he pursues other interests.
17. A litigant lacks the parenting skills and abilities to adequately provide for minimal needs of children.

If you are the parent of an infant or pre-school age child, would you feel comfortable in letting any one of the above litigants obtain permanent legal custody of your child or even obtain unrestricted liberal visitation? In all probability, it would not be in any child's best interest regardless of the age of the child, to have to live permanently with any of the above litigants. As a mother, I for one realize how upset I would become if I thought my husband's and my son would ever be in the position of children in custody cases, and professional services were not available to advocate for his needs and rights. If you would object to your child residing with the above litigants, then I am convinced you should begin to realize or already realize the reason court-ordered custody investigations are essential and should be mandatory in contested custody cases. Professional intervention could result in preventive services offered that would help prevent potential future child abuse or neglect. The service could also help insure that the child is not placed with a litigant where the child would be in potential risk of harm. Professional intervention also has the potential of helping contribute to cases being resolved out of court, as has been this author's experience in recent cases. The end result is minimal hostility, anger, and resentment..

The hypothetical examples are based on actual cases that this author has encountered during "routine" court-ordered custody investigations. Not providing a service in the custody area unless a litigant pays for the service would be analogous to an investigator responding to an alleged child abuse or neglect call by saying that the investigation will be completed only *if* the alleged perpetrator of the abuse or neglect agrees to pay for the investigation. I've found that usually the situations that warrant services the most and that have the most potential for benefiting children are situations in which litigants are either financially not able or willing to pay for needed services. Children are the innocent victims in custody cases, and they should not be denied needed services due to a parent's behavior or any other factor over which the child has no control. Children have their entire future at stake and their lives are worth professional intervention being provided to help insure that they will be permitted legally to live in the most nurturing environment possible.

A custody case pending in court is one that a professional at least knows a court decision will be made and you at least have an opportunity to offer professional input that will be an aid to the court and of benefit to children. This author contends that this service is more essential, valuable and beneficial than trying to motivate parents who have a lifestyle of living in filth, to begin having the home environment sanitary. Many persons are happy with their lifestyle, refuse to change, resent agency intervention, and many times courts will not remove children in these cases because the environment is not life-threatening and the child is so emotionally attached to the parents that he would in all probability be devastated emotionally by separation from the parents. It seems that time is better spent in providing professional services that can really have a significant impact on a child's life and one with court action pending, such as in custody litigation.

The custody area is one that is essential and certainly important enough to warrant the exploration of potential sources of funding for this area so that the quality of service delivery in this area can be improved.

Legislators are in a position to assess whether or not funding can be provided for this area—one that is important enough to warrant specialized services (at least in areas that have a fairly steady influx of contested custody cases in the courts).

This author's hope is that if sources of funding are available in the custody area, for agencies such as the Illinois Department of Children and Family Services to utilize, that legislators will be willing to utilize their expertise in obtaining needed funding for the custody area. Innocent victims in custody cases would appreciate any assistance that can be provided in helping them to reach the goal of professional services being offered in their behalf. Services offered need to be quality services provided from a knowledge base from which professional skill and expertise in the complexities of the custody area will emerge. Let's hope that children don't end up in an abusive or neglectful environment due to our failure or negligence in *not* providing quality services in custody cases.

In this author's opinion, Director Gordon Johnson is the best director the Illinois Department of Children and Family Services has ever had in the history of this agency. The quality of agency services has improved significantly under Director Johnson's leadership. Deputy Director Thomas Villiger is an outstanding deputy director with exceptional skill, knowledge, and expertise in the handling of his administrative duties. Both Director Johnson and Deputy Director Villiger are supportive of our agency's exploration of funding possibilities in the custody area and are very supportive of innovative ideas being implemented that have the potential of improving the quality of service delivery in the future in the specialized service area of contested custody.

The children in the State of Illinois are very fortunate to have dedicated, knowledgeable, caring individuals such as Director Gordon Johnson, Deputy Director Thomas Villiger, The Honorable Leo Desmond, Dr. Gordon Plumb, and Dr. Dianne Skafte, who are all willing to work with legislators in attempts to insure that available funding, existing legislation, and service delivery in the custody area is providing maximum benefits to all innocent victims of contested custody litigation.

Chapter 24

METHOD UTILIZED IN COMPLETING THE
INVESTIGATIVE CUSTODY REPORT

The method this social worker utilized in completing this Investigative Report included procedures outlined in the Investigative Custody Report Manual that this social worker wrote in 1987. Specific procedures included the following:

1. Interviewing litigants including adult members of each household.
2. Interviewing children involved in the current custody proceedings.
3. Observation of the children with both litigants including adult members of each household.
4. Interviewing collaterals in order to obtain relevant information.
5. Obtaining information from school staff in regard to school age children. (School form designed by this social worker for custody cases.)
6. Obtaining background information from litigants (information contained in a questionnaire this social worker designed.)
7. Having each litigant and any other member of each household complete forms designed to assess the extent of each litigant's focus on the needs of children and their flexibility and/or recognition of the importance of a child's developing and/or maintaining loving, positive and meaningful relationships with each parent and extended families (unless there are facts to substantiate that this plan is not in the children's best interests).

The questions utilized in interviewing litigants and children are designed to help assess the following:

1. The parental capacity of each litigant and adult member of the household.
2. A litigant's flexibility in regard to visitation with the non-custodial parent.
3. A litigant's flexibility in regard to individualizing needs of each child.
4. The extent of each litigant's focus on the needs of children rather than on their own needs.

The final step in the investigative procedure is the assessment of all the information and observations obtained during the completion of the

96

custody investigation. The assessment includes listing the major advantages and/or criteria and the main disadvantages of each litigant's situation as it relates to the best interest of the child.

MAJOR AND MINOR CRITERIA UTILIZED IN THE ASSESSMENT PHASE OF A CUSTODY INVESTIGATION

Major criteria utilized in assessing which litigant can provide a home environment that can best meet the child's needs on a permanent basis (considering the best interests of the child) follow:

(1) Psychological parent.

(2) The litigant who has been or is able to be the most active participant in performing the majority of major child care tasks (provided quality of care is acceptable) (the quantity or extent of child care involvement).

(3) The litigant who is the most actively involved in spending quality time in recreational and/or educational activities with the child (quality of child care).

(4) Continuity of relationships.

(5) Flexibility regarding visitation issues.

(6) The litigant who is the least critical and judgmental of others and who is better able and willing to encourage the child or children to have a positive, loving and meaningful relationship with the other parent and extended family.

(7) The litigant who is the more capable of focusing on the needs of the child or children rather than on the needs of the litigant (the litigant who is the least self-centered—the litigant who can individualize needs of children).

Minor criteria utilized in assessing which litigant can provide a permanent home that will be in the best interests of the child include the following:

(1) Financial resources (material advantages).

(2) Current living arrangements (including physical features of home environment or the composition of adult members of each litigant's household, which may include a mother or father figure who has no legal commitment to the litigant or children involved in the current custody proceeding).

(3) Lifestyle of litigant unless the lifestyle is adversely affecting a child in significant ways.

(4) Past immature or negative behavior of litigant unless the past behavior currently affects the litigant's parenting abilities in an adverse way or has a direct adverse effect currently on children.

(5) Child rearing practices and beliefs (unless practices and/or beliefs result in abusive, neglectful or other behavior resulting in the child being adversely affected by the child rearing techniques).

(6) Opportunities for child's involvement with extended families.

(7) Child's stated preference regarding living arrangement.

After assessing each litigant in relation to the above major and minor criteria, the litigant who offers the home environment reflecting the majority of the major criteria would in all probability offer the home which would be in the best interests of the child or children. Minor criteria are considered but there should be facts to substantiate that minor criteria adversely affect a child emotionally, physically, educationally, morally and/or medically before the more importance or significance would be placed on the minor criteria than on the major criteria. It seems evident from research and experience in the custody area that not placing the most importance and significance on major criteria can result in a child being adversely affected emotionally.

An objective and thorough assessment or evaluation by a qualified professional should result in a determination of criteria offered by each litigant. Each custody investigation or evaluation is usually quite complex and requires the time and expertise of a qualified professional to be able to assess the advantages and disadvantages of each litigant's home in relation to the major and minor criteria listed. The presence, absence or extent of each criteria present is determined in the assessment or evaluation. It should be stressed that the litigant who has the majority of major criteria as advantages to his or her home *must* also be in a position financially, emotionally, physically and intellectually to provide the educational, physical, emotional, medical and spiritual needs of the child or children and also *must* offer a safe home environment in which a child will not be neglected, physically abused or emotionally abused.

Criteria such as physical and emotional health of a litigant are important considerations only in relation to the effects on a litigant's parenting abilities. All major and minor criteria are assessed in relation to the effects each factor has on a litigant's parenting ability. The child and his needs is the central focus around which the investigation and evaluation evolves.

It is essential that each custody investigation and evaluation be conducted in an objective manner with interview questions, observations and other methods utilized designed to assess each litigant's home in relation to the absence or presence of each major or minor criteria. All criteria utilized are significant in assessing factors relating to the quality of care provided by each litigant and each litigant's ability to meet a child's educational, physical, emotional, medical and spiritual needs. Each child's needs should be individualized to take into consideration any specific needs one particular child may have that would not necessarily be applicable to another child. For example, there are minimal standards considered acceptable in each area, but if one child has a medical problem requiring daily medical care, that care must be provided in addition to the routine medical care all children need.

Any method utilized in conducting custody investigations or evaluations needs to meet the following criteria:

(1) It must be as fair and objective as possible.

(2) It must be a method that can be duplicated in each evaluation or investigation conducted.

(3) It must be designed to assess the major and minor criteria already listed as being ones to consider in trying to assess which litigant's home could best meet the needs of the child or children involved in the custody litigation.

(4) It must be a method that can uniformly be provided by any qualified professional who possesses the knowledge, skills, and expertise in the specialized area of custody. Obviously each professional involved in completing custody evaluations or investigations (psychologists, preferably MSW, CSW or ACSW social workers, psychiatrists or other master's level mental health professionals) utilizes its own specialized methods applicable to its own professional area of expertise.

Chapter 25

INVESTIGATIVE CUSTODY REPORT

Re: Doe vs. Doe
Docket Number: 77-G-77
Custody County Court

Child: Gordon Doe
Born: July 7, 1977

Father: Robert Doe
43 Seventh Street
Newton, Illinois 62448

Mother: Robin Doe
7437 Washington Street
Olney, Illinois

This report is submitted in accordance with an Order of the Court to investigate both parties relative to the custody of one minor child. To this worker's knowledge, no hearing date has been set.

I. METHOD USED: The method utilized by this worker in completing this Investigative Custody Report is explained in some detail in the attached sheet. (Please refer to the chapter "Completed Investigative Custody Report"—Method and Criteria Utilized.)

II. CONTACTS WITH LITIGANTS, INCLUDING GORDON:

05/26/87   In-person interview with Gordon Doe at
Newton Grade School in Newton, Illinois.

05/26/87   In-person interview with Robert Doe in the office.

05/28/87   Home visit and in-person interview with
Robin Doe.

06/08/87   Office visit and in-person interview with
Robin Doe.

06/08/87   Unannounced home visit and in-person
interview with Robin Doe. Worker also

talked to Robin's father and mother on
this particular home visit.

06/11/87   Unannounced home visit to Robert Doe's
home. In-person interview with Robert
Doe. Worker also saw Gordon before this
visit terminated.

06/15/87   Home visit and in-person interview with
Robert Doe.

06/15/87   Interview with Gordon on the front porch
of his house.

06/15/87   Interview with Gordon at McDonald's in
Newton, Illinois.

06/16/87   An unannounced attempted home visit at
Robin Doe's house.

III. CONTACTS WITH COLLATERALS: This worker interviewed
the following collaterals in regard to this custody case:

Judge Leo Desmond
Dr. Gordon Plumb
State Central Registry— in order to have Gordon soundexed
in order to check for any indicated
reports of abuse or neglect.
Grimes Westford
Pharmacist, Rusty Dunbar
Department of Public Aid Staff in McLeansboro, Illinois]
Christine Turnipseed
Allan Stuck
Robin's father
Robin's mother
County School Counselor, Charlene Vaughn
County School Nurse, Ruth Adams
Gordon Doe's barber, Millard Winters
Jon Westfall, Carmi Police (gun expert)
Robert H. Rath, Attorney at Law
Bruce D. Stewart, Attorney at Law
Michael V. Oshel, Attorney at Law
Aaron Ray Lindley
David Aaron Lindley

The five page collateral questionnaire forms were sent to the following persons:

Dr. Marie Childers	Dr. Olive Haynes
Lisa Childers	Dr. Elliott Partridge
Dr. Paul Lorenz	Loretta Gooch
Darla Partridge	Director Gordon Johnson
Lynn Downen	Delores Lorenz
Alan Downen, State's Attorney	Thomas Villiger
Dianne Skafte	

As of this particular date, none of the collateral forms have been returned to our office.

IV. OBSERVATIONS DURING VISITS TO THE HOME OF ROBERT DOE: This worker's observations at the home of Robert Doe during both announced and unannounced visits included the following observations:

1. The children related well to both Robert and his wife, Clara.
2. The children were neat and clean in appearance.
3. The children were dressed appropriately for the weather conditions.
4. The children were polite, asked permission to go places and minded well.
5. Gordon was observed talking spontaneously, laughing, smiling, and he appeared to be very happy and content in his father's home.
6. Gordon was affectionate with his dad on more than one occasion during the visits.
7. During visits to Robert's home, I heard both Gordon and Charlie spontaneously refer to Clara as "mom."
8. Robert's home was neat and clean on announced and unannounced visits.
9. Robert's home was adequately furnished.
10. Robert has a three bedroom house. Gordon and Charlie share a bedroom, each having their own bed.

V. OBSERVATIONS DURING THE HOME VISIT TO ROBIN DOE'S RESIDENCE: During the home visit to Robin Doe's residence, this worker observed that Robin's current living arrangement consists of a modern doublewide trailer that consists of three bedrooms (one of which Robin indicated is Gordon's), a living room, kitchen area, dining room and two bathrooms. Robin indicated that the couches also make into beds. The trailer was neat and clean in appearance and adequately furnished for the type of living arrangement that it is. Robin also showed this worker some of Gordon's clothes that were in the closet.

VI. SIGNIFICANT INFORMATION FROM INTERVIEWS WITH GORDON: During this worker's first interview with Gordon at Newton Grade School, the interview lasted approximately one and one fourth hours. This worker discussed with Gordon the purpose of the interview as well as discussing what it means to tell the truth. This worker stressed to Gordon that my main concern was him and his welfare and that I wanted him to answer each question as honestly as he possibly could, being sure to provide me with his own feelings and ideas in regard to each question. This worker asked Gordon approximately 18 questions from the manual that this worker wrote in regard to completing custody investigations. This worker also utilized two completion forms for children that are utilized in custody investigations.

During this worker's second interview with Gordon, approximately thirty-seven questions were asked of Gordon including approximately seven questions from the completion forms that were seven identical questions asked during this worker's first interview with Gordon. Some of the questions asked of Gordon included various situations in which only one parent could be present and Gordon was asked to select the parent that he would prefer to be with him in each given situation. Open ended questions were also utilized in which the answer did not have to include a choice between parents or even a specification that the answer needed to include a parent. Other questions asked related to discipline in each home, meals in each home, recreational activities in each home, lifestyle of each litigant, and other questions related to the allegations or concerns expressed by the litigants.

Gordon's answers to questions that asked for a specific choice to be made between his parents in different situations as well as open ended questions that did not specify that the answer include either parent consistently provided answers in which he gave his father as being the answer in both the first and second interview with Gordon. There were approximately fourteen specific questions asked of Gordon in the first interview in which his answer was his father. This worker cannot recall any question in either the first or second interview with Gordon that was answered with the answer being his mother. Specific examples include the question #9 on the completion form—If I were in the hospital and only one parent could stay in the room with me, I would choose _____ to be with me. Gordon's answer to this particular question was "dad—I would feel a lot safer." Question #10—If I could go to any place I chose for a day (such as to Six Flags) and I could only take one of my parents, I would want to go with _____. Gordon's answer was his dad because he hardly gets to see him. Question #11—The parent that would be the most willing to help me if I got in trouble would be _____. Gordon's answer was his dad. Question #16—I am really looking forward to the day when _____. Gordon's answer was, "I go to court so I can be with my dad." Question #17—"When I get out of school, I would like to _____. Gordon's answer was to go with his dad. I would feel happy. On completion form two—question #2—If I feel real sad, I would feel better talking to _____. Gordon's answer was his dad. Question #5—If I got into trouble, I would want to talk to _____. Gordon's answer was his dad. Question #6—If I had a big secret, I would feel more comfortable discussing it with _____. Gordon's answer was his dad. Question #10—If I felt unhappy, I would want to be with _____. Gordon's answer was his dad. Gordon did indicate that even if he got to see his father frequently, his answer to this question would still be the same. Question #16—If I were sick I would want to be with _____. Gordon's answer was his dad. Question #17—The person who makes me feel the most worthwhile and important is _____. Gordon's answer was his dad. When some of these same specific questions were repeated in the second interview with Gordon, his answers were the same in terms of his answers being his dad. In Gordon's answer to the question if he had a preference with regard to his permanent living arrangement, in both the first and second interviews, Gordon indicated that he did have a preference and that his preference was to live with his dad on a permanent basis but he would like to visit his mom.

On completion form two for children, one particular question was significant in terms of Gordon's answer. The question was #1—If I won $500, I would want to _____. Gordon's answer in the first interview was "give it to my dad." The significant part of Gordon's answer seems that Gordon included his dad in the answer but did not mention his mom.

Gordon did indicate he feels under the most pressure regarding the custody issue when he is with his mom due to the pressure he feels his mother is putting on him in terms of the custody issue.

Gordon indicated it would be easier to deal with his parent's divorce if his dad would get to spend more time with him.

Gordon also indicated in the first interview that it would be easier to deal with his parent's divorce if his mom would "straighten up." Gordon indicated that by his mom straightening up, he means that his mom should let him spend more time with his dad.

In Gordon's answer to the question—If you had three wishes what would they be—Gordon's first wish was to be with his dad, his second wish was to be with his dad on weekends, and his third wish was to go skating every day. Gordon indicated that he feels a lot safer and secure with his dad.

Gordon indicated that he was not unhappy with his living situation in his dad's home at the time his mom took him to live with her. Gordon indicated he was not very happy when he began living with his mom and it was not his desire to live with his mom.

In answer to the question—Is there anything about visiting your mom that makes you unhappy—Gordon indicated nothing, but I miss my dad.

Gordon indicated in this worker's second interview with him that he does not remember talking to his mom's attorney and does not remember the conversation he had with the attorney.

Gordon indicated that he asked to see his dad almost daily during the period of time he lived with his mom but his mom refused to let him visit his dad.

Gordon indicated a happiness and contentment in being back in his dad's home and did not give any current facts to indicate that he is abused, neglected or mistreated in any way.

Gordon was very concerned that his mom not know these particular answers of his to the questions as he loves his mom and does not want to hurt her feelings.

VII. AREAS COVERED DURING INTERVIEWS: The main areas covered in interviews with litigants as well as Gordon and Charlie centered around the lifestyle of the litigants, including drug and alcohol usage by the litigants as well as discipline in the home and other questions relating to allegations or areas of concern.

VIII. DEFINITION OF "CONTINUITY OF RELATIONSHIPS" AND "PSYCHOLOGICAL PARENT": This worker defines continuity of relationships as being a continuity or continuation of relationships and emotional attachments between a child and parent over an extended period of time.

This worker would define psychological parent as the parent or parent figure that the child consistently has demonstrated (either by behavior and/or verbally) the greatest emotional attachment. In other words, the psychological parent for a child is the parent or parent substitute or parent figure with whom the child has the greatest emotional attachment and has formed the greatest emotional bond. If the child's emotional attachment seems to be equal toward each parent, then each parent would be considered to be a psychological parent for the child.

IX. SPECIFIC FORMS UTILIZED: Specific forms utilized during the completion of this custody investigation included the four-page questionnaire that was completed by the litigants (and is attached to this report), a rating form, additional questions on an additional sheet including seven questions, two true/false forms, two completion forms, and an additional form regarding opportunities or experiences children could experience. This particular form relates to values.

This worker also utilized a five-page collateral form that was sent to various Newton collaterals as well as a school form that was sent to the Newton County School but as of this date has not been returned. Two completion forms for children were also utilized as well as interview questions for litigants and children outlined in this worker's investigative custody manual.

X. ASSESSMENT AND CONCLUSION: During the assessment phase of this particular custody investigation, this worker reviewed approximately fifty-two pages of handwritten notes, thirty-one pages of forms completed by litigants, as well as fifteen pages total of collateral forms which would be a total of approximately ninety-eight pages of material.

This worker's last interviews with the following persons included approximately Gordon's answers to forty-three questions, Robin's answers to approximately thirteen questions, Robert's answers to approximately thirteen questions, and Charlie's answers to approximately fifteen questions, in addition to other questions that were asked.

This worker spent approximately fourteen hours total just in in-person interviews with the litigants, Gordon and Charlie, in addition to approximately two and one-half hours interview time with collaterals, approximately twelve hours total in travel time, and approximately three to four hours total in assessment time. This worker would estimate that this particular custody investigation was completed in approximately thirty-two and one-half hours, not counting the time spent in dictation.

My research and experience in completing custody investigations during my specialization in the custody area have resulted in a belief that the major criteria attached to this report are the most important criteria to consider in assessing which home environment will be the least detrimental to the child to reside in on a permanent basis. Information outlined by Dianne Skafte (author and expert in the custody area as well as a member of a custody evaluation team in Colorado) outlines factors to consider to determine when it would be in a child's best interest for a father to obtain permanent legal custody of a child. In considering the factors outlined in Dianne Skafte's article, there are facts to substantiate that Robert Doe meets the criteria outlined in Dianne Skafte's article.

This worker's assessment includes the following:

1. Gordon loves both parents.
2. Both parents love Gordon.
3. Gordon needs to be able to have positive loving relationships with both parents and extended families.
4. Gordon should not be put under pressure emotionally by either parent or family member.
5. Gordon definitely wants to live with his father on a permanent basis.
6. In my almost two years of specializing in completing custody investigations, I cannot ever recall interviewing any child who demonstrated a greater emotional attachment for a parent than Gordon does for his father.
7. It is in Gordon's best interest if he can live with his dad on a permanent basis.
8. Gordon's sibling relationship with Charlie is important to Gordon.
9. Robin has demonstrated a lack of focus on Gordon's needs and a lack of understanding his need to be with his dad (emotional attachment).
10. Robin, in essence, kidnapped Gordon against his will and kept him from seeing his dad for almost a year which demonstrates a total lack of concern for Gordon's needs and/or emotional attachment for his father.
11. There are no facts to substantiate that Gordon has been abused or neglected in his dad's home.
12. It would be traumatic for Gordon if he were taken away from his dad again.
13. Robin, her father and mother have placed Gordon under pressure emotionally by questioning him in regard to the custody issue.
14. Robin has not been honest in some situations—such as with school staff in Jasper County in regard to Gordon's name, Gordon's attending Jasper County Schools but not residing in the Jasper County area, and has not mentioned her involvement with the police on her questionnaire for this custody report. These are some but not all of the examples in which this worker believes Robin has not been honest.
15. Robert is basically honest, even if information was negative about him. Robert does not try "to put on an act" just for my benefit. For example, during one of this worker's visits to Robert's home, Robert was in the middle of eating a meal when the worker arrived.

Robert did not immediately stop eating as many persons have done during this worker's experience in completing custody investigations of others who are in a similar situation. Robert instead indicated they would be done eating within a short period of time. Another example is Robert did not "give in" to Gordon in Gordon's requests in front of me if Robert thought Gordon's requests were not appropriate.

16. The disadvantages to Robin's home far outweigh the advantages to Gordon.
17. The advantages of Robert's home far outweigh the disadvantages for Gordon.

Robin, Robert and Clara all three are currently unemployed, all have financial limitations, and all have exhibited negative behaviors in the past such as drinking alcoholic beverages; however, there are no facts to substantiate that Robert's lifestyle has interfered adversely with his ability to assume child care responsibilities or that the children have been affected adversely, neglected, or abused as a result of the lifestyle. This was even substantiated by this worker's interview with Charlie Doe.

XI. ADVANTAGES TO GORDON IF HE RESIDES ON A PERMANENT BASIS WITH HIS MOTHER, ROBIN DOE:

1. Quality of care good with the help of Robin's extended family.
2. Robin has expressed flexibility in regard to visitation issues although she has denied visitation rights to Gordon in the past to visit his dad.
3. Robin has indicated that she tries to encourage a positive relationship between Gordon and Robert.

XII. DISADVANTAGES TO GORDON IF HE RESIDES ON A PERMANENT BASIS WITH HIS MOM, ROBIN DOE:

1. Robin is *not* the psychological parent for Gordon.
2. Robin has *not* been the parent who has assumed the major responsibilities for child care tasks for Gordon since Gordon's birth—by Robin's own admission, she did not assume child care responsibilities.
3. The continuity of relationships criteria does *not* apply to Robin.
4. Robin has demonstrated a lack of concern or focus on Gordon's needs (Robin has not individualized the needs of Gordon).
5. Robin's current living arrangements are not appropriate for a long term permanent living arrangement.
6. Financial limitations.
7. There is a possibility that Robin will not have much time with Gordon in the event she obtains employment outside this area (if Gordon resides with Robin's father and mother).
8. Robin is not honest in some recent situations.

9. Robin tends to believe negative information in regard to Robert without obtaining verification of information based on facts.
10. Robin has demonstrated a lack of stability in her living situation during the time Gordon was with her (her various moves to different states and Gordon's enrolling in several different schools).

XIII. ADVANTAGES TO GORDON IF HE RESIDES ON A PERMANENT BASIS WITH HIS FATHER, ROBERT DOE:

1. The continuity of relationships criteria is met by Robert's home.
2. Robert is the psychological parent for Gordon.
3. Robert meets the criteria in regard to quality of child care—specifically in regard to his involvement in recreational activities with the children and his involvement in child care.
4. Robert has expressed a flexibility in regard to visitation issues if problems do not arise regarding visitation that would be detrimental—in the past there have been some problems in regard to Robert's past refusal to permit visitation based on problems that arose.
5. Robert is nonjudgmental and able to encourage Gordon to have a positive relationship with his mom.
6. Robert's home meets the criteria of quantity of care or extent of child care involvement.
7. Robert is able to individualize needs of children and focus on the children's needs.
8. There is both a mother and father figure in Robert's home.
9. Sibling relationships are important to Gordon and he would be able to maintain his relationship with Charlie on an almost daily or at least weekly basis in the event he can reside in his dad's home on a permanent basis.
10. Robert does not put pressure emotionally on Gordon regarding the custody situation as Robin and her family do.

XIV. DISADVANTAGES TO GORDON IF HE RESIDES IN HIS FATHER'S HOME ON A PERMANENT BASIS:

1. Clara has no legal commitment to Robert, Charlie or Gordon.
2. Financial limitations.
3. Robert and Clara at times have demonstrated poor judgment in situations and some of the factors in their past lifestyle might not provide a good role model for children.

It is evident that there are advantages and disadvantages to both litigant's homes. This particular custody case is quite complex, and with the varying perceptions of the allegations, it becomes difficult to arrive at a definite decision in regard to the truth of some of the allegations related during this investigation. However, based on all the information and observations this worker obtained during the completion of this custody investigation, the above assessment was completed after not only a thorough investigation but also after much thought.

In closing, the weight of the evidence based on information and observations during the completion of this custody investigation, would indicate that Robert's home offers more advantages to Gordon than Robin's home would.

Dictated by:

Mary E. Lindley, MSW, CSW
Child Welfare Specialist
Harrisburg Field Office

MEL/ds

Chapter 26

INVESTIGATIVE REPORT

Re: Samantha Sun
Born: July 7, 1983

Sun vs. Sun
Docket Number: 77-7-77
Custody County Court

Mother: Edie Sun
           77 Washington Street
           Newton, Illinois 62448

Father: Evan Sun
           77 Lincoln Street
           Newton, Illinois 62448

This report is submitted in accordance with an order of the court to investigate both parties relative to the issue of visitation. To this worker's knowledge the hearing date has not been set for this matter.

(I.) Method Utilized in Completing This Investigation: The method this worker utilized in completing this investigative report included procedures outlined in the Investigative Custody report Manual that this worker wrote this year. These procedures included obtaining background information in regard to Edie and Evan Sun, interviewing parties to this current court proceeding including making home visits to Edie and Evan's homes, interviewing Samantha, obtaining medical information in regard to Samantha's medical condition (cystic fibrosis), interviewing collaterals who were asked to relate relevant information to this matter, completing the final report which included an in-depth assessment of factors relevant to any of the child custody proceedings.

Since the issue resulting in the initiation of court action resulted from disagreements in regard to visitation rather than from an issue in regard to the contested custody, this worker did utilize questions in interviews geared toward a thorough assessment of the following: (1) Problems regarding current visitation; (2) Edie's reasons for being opposed to Samantha having extended visitation with Evan; (3) Medical considerations due to Samantha having cystic fibrosis; (4) Advantages and/or disadvantages to Samantha having opportunities for increased visitation with Evan; and, (5) Current living arrangements and situation of Edie, Evan and Samantha.

(II.) Summary of In-Person Contacts with Edie, Evan and Samantha: This worker has had the following in-person contacts with Edie, Evan and Samantha:

7/7/87	Home visit to Evan's home.
7/7/87	Home visit to Edie's home.
7/17/87	Unannounced home visit to Evan's home.
7/18/87	Home visit to Evan's home. During this visit, this worker observed Samantha's interaction with Evan.
7/18/87	This worker did talk alone with Samantha before and after her visit with her dad. During this time, worker provided the transportation for Samantha's visit with her father.
7/19/87	Home visit to Evan Sun's home.
7/19/87	Home visit to Edie Sun's home. Edie, Samantha and Edie's fiance, Rick Doe, were present.

(III.) Contacts with Collaterals: This worker interviewed the following collaterals:

Bob Turnipseed
Diane Boien (Social Worker/Richland Memorial Hospital)
Bob Gile
Deputy Ed Miller
Dr. John O'Keefe
Bob Allison
Edie Lovan
Evan Lovan
Willie Nelson
Maven Turnipseed
Mary Ann Gile
Bernie Hoffman
Bob Hoffman
Dick Moon

Sam Trefts
Earl Faulkner (Division of Services for Crippled
    Children's Worker)
Debbie Greer (Rehabilitation Teacher)
LeRoy Anderson
Doris Anderson
State Central Registry
Barb Posten (Department of Public Aid Worker)
Stephanie Vaughn

(IV.) Observations During This Worker's Home Visits to Evan Sun's Apartment (including this worker's unannounced visit): In general, Evan's apartment was neat and clean in appearance. It is adequately furnished. The apartment is a one bedroom apartment but there is a couch that makes into a bed and there is also a rollaway bed. Even during this worker's unannounced visit, the apartment was never filthy or unsanitary.

In this worker's observations of Samantha with Evan, this worker would summarize the interaction as one in which both persons interacted and related well with each other. Evan participated in activities with Samantha and talked with Samantha during much of the visit. Evan was affectionate with Samantha. At the end of the visit Samantha was affectionate with Evan and she told Evan that she loved him. At Samantha's request, Evan did purchase a Happy Meal at Hardee's for Samantha. This worker did observe Evan giving Samantha her medication before Samantha began eating the meal.

Evan spent time talking with Samantha in attempting to answer many of Samantha's questions. Evan showed Samantha a calculator, a tape recorder, a braille book and filled out adoption papers for Samantha's Cabbage Patch doll that was purchased for Samantha by Evan.

Prior to Samantha's visit with her dad ending, Evan's wife, Eve, participated in educational activities with Samantha. Samantha smiled and laughed during much of the visit and appeared to be happy and relaxed. Evan spent time in activities with Samantha and in this worker's observations, Evan related well with his daughter. Both Evan and Eve interacted in a positive manner with Samantha and both assumed responsibility for her supervision.

(V.) Summary of This Worker's Interview With Samantha: Before and after Samantha's visit with her dad, this worker talked with Samantha during the time this worker provided transportation for Samantha from the

Department of Children and Family Services offices to Evan's apartment and from Evan's apartment back to the Department of Children and Family Services office.

Samantha indicated that she wanted to visit with her dad on this particular day. According to Samantha, her mother sometimes makes her (Samantha) cry because Samantha's mother will not let her see her dad even when she asks to see him. Samantha indicated that she enjoys visiting her dad and that she would like to be able to see him on weekends, holidays and during the summer. Samantha related positive feelings in regard to Eve as well.

(VI.) Medical Considerations: Samantha is considered by medical staff to be one of the much better cystic fibrosis children. At this point, Samantha's health is good and her nutritional state is good. Samantha is to be treated like any other child as much as possible. When Samantha is school age, she will be expected to attend a regular school and there are no real restrictions in terms of her activities. It is this worker's understanding from talking with medical staff that they would have no objections to Samantha's having extended visitation with her father as long as Evan can manage the daily medical care required.

Daily medical care that is required for Samantha include the following:

1) Pancrease capsules are needed, two before each meal or snack. It is critical that this particular medication be given as directed on a daily basis.

2) Proventil inhaler — one puff every six hours as needed.

3) There should be no smoking around Samantha.

4) Postural drainage completed every day at least once and possibly more than once a day as a preventive measure.

5) Samantha should not have any out-of-town trips out of this area unless approved by Dr. O'Keefe and other medical staff.

The above daily medical care is typical of care required for numerous children who have cystic fibrosis. In addition to the above daily medical care of Samantha that is essential, there might also be occasions when Samantha needs other medication in addition to the above.

(VII.) Some of Edie's Concerns in Addition to This Worker's Assessment of Each Concern: C. = Edie's Concern A. = Worker's Assessment of Concern.

1. C. — In general, Evan is not a responsible person.

   A. — Documentation from collaterals indicate that Evan has made significant, positive improvements within this past year in regard to his attitude and behavior. Some of the indications of Evan's positive behavior include his cooperating with his probation officer, Evan's voluntarily attending Alcoholics Anonymous Meetings on a weekly basis, Evan's voluntarily becoming involved in counseling and the fact that Evan has no new violations this year.

2. C. — The only reason Evan initiated court action in trying to get increased visitation with Samantha is due to Eve's instigation.

   A. — It would be this worker's assessment based on information from collaterals as well as based on interview and observation of Evan that he very much wants increased visitation with his daughter. Some indications of Evan's love and concern for Samantha include not only his initiation of court action in regard to this matter but also includes the following: Evan obtained an air conditioner for his apartment due to the medical necessity of air conditioning being provided for Samantha. Evan attended the cystic fibrosis classes with Edie after Samantha was born. Evan helped to obtain SSI benefits for Samantha; Evan has read material regarding cystic fibrosis and is willing to go to Olney, Illinois, in order that an assessment can be made by medical staff regarding his understanding of cystic fibrosis as well as his ability to deal with medical aspects of daily care of Samantha and the fact that Evan obtained medication that Samantha needs on a daily basis so that it would be available for Samantha during visits.

3. C. — Evan's and Eve's apartment is filthy.

   A. — Information from collaterals as well as observations of this worker of Evan's and Eve's apartment indicated that the apartment in general is clean and neat in appearance and is certainly sanitary and is never filthy.

4. C. — Due to Eve's current eye problem she is not able to provide adequate supervision to children.

   A. — Eve does have a condition diagnosed as retinitis pigmentosa and cataracts on one eye. The retinitis pigmentosa affects field vision and also causes night blindness. Information obtained from Debbie Greer (Eve's rehabilitation teacher) indicate that Debbie has observed Eve with children and Debbie has no question about Eve's ability to monitor and adequately supervise children. Eve has demonstrated skills to be a mother and Eve compensates well for her limitations. Eve realizes her limitations. She is realistic in regard to her abilities and she is cautious and uses good judgment in dealing with children. Debbie Greer also related that her supervisor and his wife are totally blind; they successfully raised their children and are now in the process of babysitting for grandchildren on occasions.

5. C. — Evan is not knowledgeable in regard to medical care needed for Samantha.

A. — Evan and Eve both showed this worker several pamphlets and literature in regard to cystic fibrosis that they indicated they have read. Evan also showed this worker a chart on the twelve steps of postural drainage. Both Evan and Eve indicate in their discussion that they do understand cystic fibrosis and are aware of daily care that is required. They are both willing to go to Olney and have their understanding and abilities to deal with daily medical care requirements for Samantha assessed by medical staff at the Olney Hospital.

(VIII.) Significant Inconsistencies Noted in Regard to Edie's Expressed Beliefs: The following are significant inconsistencies noted in regard to Edie's expressed beliefs. The following inconsistencies would tend to raise serious questions as to the validity of some of Edie's concerns:

1. Edie indicated that she thinks Evan still may be drinking alcoholic beverages and smoking "pot." Edie also indicated there is a possibility that Eve was smoking "pot."

   Edie admitted to this worker that in the past she has drunk alcoholic beverages excessively herself on occasions and has also smoked "pot." She has even received in-patient treatment for alcohol and drug related problems.

2. Edie indicated that Evan's car needs repairs such as needing new tires, seat belts in the back, and the turn signals need to be repaired.

   Evan provided transportation for Edie and Samantha to Olney, Illinois, recently when Samantha was hospitalized. Edie indicated that Samantha does not always wear seat belts because sometimes she likes to ride sitting on a person's lap.

3. Edie does not acknowledge the possibility that Evan and/or Eve could have made positive changes in their behavior.

   Interestingly enough, Edie admitted that her own past behavior on at least one occasion resulted in one of her neighbors calling

Department of Children and Family Services to report Edie's behavior out of a concern for Samantha. In discussing some of Edie's own behavior in the past, she indicated that it is important that persons learn from their mistakes. In fact, she believes she has become a better person partly as a result of lessons she learned from her past mistakes.

4. Edie is concerned that Evan is not knowledgeable in regard to the daily required medical care of Samantha. Edie indicated to this worker that the postural drainage is not done on a daily basis by Edie but is only done when Samantha is sick, such as having symptoms or requiring additional medication. Edie indicated that Samantha should not have certain foods such as fried foods although sometimes she does permit Samantha to eat fried foods.

(IX.) Worker's Assessment and Conclusions: This worker's assessment and conclusions are based on information and observations obtained during this worker's completion of this investigation. It might be noted that this worker spent approximately eleven hours total in interviews with Edie, Samantha, Evan and/or Eve, in addition to the time spent in contacts with collaterals and in completing the assessment and dictating the report. Completing the assessment consisted of reviewing approximately forty pages of notes. This worker would estimate the time spent in the completion of this investigation as consisting of at least twenty-two to twenty-five hours.

This worker's assessment includes the following:

1. A mutually agreed upon place for visitation between Edie and Evan never occurred.
2. Evan loves Samantha and Samantha loves Evan.
3. Samantha likes to visit Evan.
4. Evan and Eve would not do anything intentionally to hurt Samantha.
5. Evan and Eve have made significant positive changes, particularly since July, 1982, which has been verified by collaterals.
6. There is no medical reason Samantha cannot visit Evan for extended visits at the Housing Project.
7. There is no medical reason Samantha should not be permitted to play with other children during regular visitation.
8. There is no reason Eve should not participate in Evan's visitation with Samantha unless there are facts to substantiate that Eve's

relationship with Samantha would be harmful to Samantha in some way.

9. Children's visitations with non-custodial parents are beneficial to children if visitation with the non-custodial parent is liberal visitation, in general, unless there are facts to indicate the non-custodial parent would be abusive, neglectful or that the liberal visitation would adversely affect a child in some way.

10. It is important for Samantha to have positive relationships with both parents and extended families. Samantha has as much right to have an opportunity to have a positive relationship with her step-mother as she would have a right to have a positive relationship with a step-father in the future.

11. Evan, Eve and Edie all need to work together for the benefit of Samantha.

12. The focus of everyone should be on Samantha's needs and on helping Samantha to strengthen her relationship with both parents and extended families.

13. Children of Samantha's age would benefit by spending long weekends, holiday time and blocks of summer vacation with non-custodial parents.

It is this worker's assessment that Edie's resentment interferes with her ability to focus on Samantha's needs in regard to the visitation issue. Evan and Eve expressed more concern for Samantha's needs and feelings during this investigation than Edie. There is data available to suggest that Edie is not focusing on Samantha's needs, but instead is being self-centered.

This worker's main concern in regard to any extended visitation of Samantha with Evan would be that Evan and Eve are able to deal with the medical aspects of Samantha's care on a daily basis. As indicated, Evan and Eve both plan to have medical staff in Olney, Illinois, assess their understanding and ability to deal with medical aspects of Samantha's care in regard to the cystic fibrosis.

If Samantha has extended visitations with Evan, medical assessment could be completed before and after Samantha's visitation.

In conclusion, this worker did not find out any facts during this investigation to indicate that Evan and Eve would place Samantha in any situation where she would be abused, neglected or affected adversely by extended visitations. Based on information and observations obtained during this investigation, it would seem that Samantha would benefit by extended visitations with her father and step-mother.

Mary E. Lindley, MSW, CSW
Harrisburg Field Office

MEL:ds

Date:

THE OBSERVATION AND ASSESSMENT PORTION ONLY OF AN INVESTIGATIVE CUSTODY REPORT IN REGARD TO VISITATION

This court investigation was ordered primarily to investigate the father's home environment and its suitability for visits as well as his ability to care for the minor child while exercising visitation privileges.

I. Major Concerns: The father's threats to take the child and leave the area; father's excessive drinking of alcoholic beverages; past aggressive behavior of the father toward others and past criminal charges against the father; potential dangers in the home environment; and lack of adequate household furnishings for a toddler that would be needed for overnight visitation or visits lasting for an extended period of time.

II. Potential Hazards in Regard to Visitation: In this worker's assessment, the following is a list of potential hazards that would be present in the father's apartment. The potential hazards listed would be particularly important in view of the child's age (a toddler).

1. The back porch is in need of repair.
2. The front porch is in need of repair (four fairly large holes in the floor of the porch).
3. There are items outside the house in the yard and on the back porch that a child could easily get hurt on such as a screen, battery, saw, other tools, and a fishing pole. Two dogs, and four cats are also outside the house most of the time.
4. The wood-burning heating stove in the living room (during cold weather) is easily accessible for the child to touch while crawling on the floor.
5. The house is not child proof (such as locks on cabinets). There are items in the bathroom such as shaving lotion, etc. that a child might be able to reach easily if adequate supervision was not provided.

In summary, the father's house would be appropriate for short visits provided the child was given constant adequate supervision at all times.

III. Worker's Assessments and Conclusions: This worker's assessment would include the following:

1. The father and child love each other and benefit from visitation.
2. The child would benefit by spending time alone with his father such as playing in the park.
3. The father would not do anything intentionally to hurt his son.
4. The father is highly motivated to do whatever the court requests or requires to be able to have visitation with his son (such as using a car seat, getting a high chair, etc.).
5. Due to the child's age, the father's current living arrangements and the father's work schedule, it would not seem appropriate or in the child's best interest for him to be at his dad's for any overnight visitation or weekend visits until he is older.
6. The father's home would seem suitable for visits, such as on the father's day off work for part of a day provided he provides close supervision of his son at all times during the visitation and insures that the environment is safe during the visitation periods, (including the physical surroundings and the behavior of any person who is present during the visitation).

ASSESSMENT PORTION ONLY OF A COURT REPORT IN REGARD TO VISITATION

In talking with both litigants, it seems that the current visitation schedule that was set up temporarily has been working satisfactorily without any apparent problem. This worker's assessment in regard to the visitation issue would include the following:

1. It is beneficial to the child to have regularly scheduled visitations with his father.
2. The father would not intentionally do anything to hurt his son.
3. The father and his family seem to genuinely love the child and want to spend time with him.
4. The father did not take child development courses or parenting classes in school and obviously due to his age has had limited opportunities in regard to assuming child care responsibility for a child of his son's age; however, he believes he is capable of assum-

ing child care responsibilities for his son and is willing to ask for assistance if needed in regard go any problems or concerns that may arise.

5. The father demonstrated an ability during the scheduled visit in handling some of the child care tasks. This worker observed the father's interaction with his son during the pre-arranged scheduled two hour visit.

6. The father's visits with his son would be beneficial to the child if a visiting schedule were set up in a manner that would take into consideration the child's age and developmental needs such as would be reflected in the attached article written by Dr. Dianne Skafte (who is a Custody Evaluator, author of a book and articles in regard to custody, and considered to be an expert in the custody area). Short, frequent visits would be beneficial for a child of the age of the one this report is about. It might be noted that overnight visits are not indicated or recommended for a child the age of this boy (as indicated in the attached article). However, as the child approaches three years old, overnight visits become important and beneficial experiences.

In summary, this worker did not find out any facts during the completion of this Investigative Report that would indicate that the father's having liberal visitation privileges with his son would not be in the child's best interest or beneficial to him as long as the visiting schedule takes into consideration the child's age and developmental needs, and the father provides a safe home environment for his son. There are no facts currently available to indicate that the father would demonstrate any behavior during visitations that would be detrimental to a child. The father's motivation to learn appropriate child care skills, his willingness to ask for help when needed, and his relatives living within close proximity and being available to offer assistance as needed are further factors that should help insure that visits will be beneficial for both the father and son.

Mary E. Lindley, MSW, CSW
Harrisburg Field Office

MEL:shs

Date:

APPENDIX SECTION

Re: _____ Custody

_____ Court No.

_____ County

Dear

Please complete the enclosed form related to a child custody proceeding at your earliest convenience and return the completed form to our office at the above address. If you have any questions regarding the information requested, please do not hesitate to notify me.

After receiving the completed form from you, I will plan to make a home visit and begin the custody investigation ordered by the court.

Very truly yours,

Mary E. Lindley, MSW, CSW
Harrisburg Field Office

MEL:ds
enclosure
Date mailed:

FORM TO BE COMPLETED BY PERSONS
INVOLVED IN CHILD CUSTODY LITIGATION

(Relevant Information Related to a Child Custody Proceeding)

Please answer all questions in this questionnaire as it relates to you, your children, and any person who is currently part of your household.

Names and birthdates of children involved in current custody proceeding:

Court number and county of jurisdiction:

Name of person wanting custody of above-named child or children:

Address:

Telephone Number:

Directions to home:

Legal name (wife's maiden):

Name of family physician:

Present situation: (State your reason for wanting custody of above child or children. Use additional sheets if necessary.)

Family composition: (List names, birthdates and birthplaces of all persons currently residing in your home; include relationship of each person to you.)

Current living arrangements: (Please list number of bedrooms and list other rooms in home.)

Length of time at above address:

Are you currently renting or do you own your home:

Education: List highest grade completed for each adult member of household; list grade in school, name of school and school address for each school age child.

Health: (List current state of health of each person in the household. If any medical problems, please specify type of problem, including any medications taken.)

Employment: (If employed, list employer's name, address, present occupation and length of time on present job.)

If not presently employed, please list previous employment:

Income: (List amount of current gross monthly income and source of income.)

Marital history: (List current marital status, list dates of all marriages, including dates of divorces, deaths or separations.)

Interests and activities: (List current interests and activities.)

List religious preference, if any, name and address of church attended on a regular basis:

List any involvement with the police of you or any member of your household, including any court convictions or charges:

Describe each child involved in current custody litigation:

List advantages and disadvantages to the child or children if you were to obtain legal custody:

List discipline methods utilized by you:

List your perception of the most important needs of children:

What are your main strengths as a parent or parent substitute:

What do you consider to be your main weaknesses as a parent or parent substitute:

List your plans for child care in the event you obtain legal custody of the child or children involved:

Please list names, addresses and phone numbers of persons you would like worker to contact who would have relevant information in regard to custody matter:

_____

Signature of person completing form

_____

(Date Completed)

APPOINTMENT LETTER

Date _____

(Address)

Dear

I would like to meet with you in your home on _____ at approximately _____. Please plan for my interview with you to last approximately two hours.

During the above-scheduled visit, I will begin my custody investigation.

If for any reason you are unable to meet with me on the above-scheduled date and time, please notify me as soon as possible at the above address or telephone number so that we can schedule another appointment.

Unless I hear from you prior to the date of my scheduled visit, I will plan to see you as indicated above.

Very truly yours,

Mary E. Lindley

SUMMARY OF CUSTODY INVESTIGATION PROCEDURES AND AGREEMENT TO COOPERATE IN INVESTIGATION

The custody investigation procedures usually include the following: each litigant's completing a questionnaire with social history information; investigator conducting home visits; interviews with child or children involved in custody issue if child is five years old or older; investigators observing each litigant with child or children; litigant's completion of forms; child's completion of forms if old enough to complete forms or to be interviewed regarding questions on forms; collaterals with relevant information may be contacted; or, other information may be obtained such as medical reports if beneficial or relevant in understanding custody issues.

If another Department of Children and Family Services Child Welfare Specialist or any other professional has relevant information concerning my family, I give my permission for relevant information to be shared between the other professional and the custody investigator.

I understand the above procedures are part of a custody investigation.

I agree to cooperate with the above procedures.

I agree to give my written consent for collateral contacts determined to be relevant if requested.

I further understand that the above procedures are utilized in order to help the investigator in assessing parenting abilities of litigants, the needs of the child, and the seven major criteria considered by the investigator to be important in any custody investigation.

I understand that I may obtain a copy of the seven major criteria at my request.

I understand that confidentiality of information obtained during this investigation *cannot* be guaranteed due to the nature of a custody proceeding. If any attorney or judge involved in this case requests to look at the investigator's file, this request will be honored. If the investigator testifies at any court hearing regarding this case, information obtained during interviews or other information in the investigator's file can be revealed during testimony.

All procedures will be followed with the goal of the child's welfare as being the primary consideration.

I understand that after the written report is sent to the judge and attorneys, the investigator is willing to discuss the report with me at my request.

I understand the above procedures and agree to cooperate with the investigation procedures requested.

I have either read the above information myself or it has been read to me.

Please circle either do or do not to indicate your preference. I do/do not want a copy of the seven major criteria.

_____

Signature of Litigant

_____

Signature of Witness   (Date)

_____

(Date)

STATEMENT OF UNDERSTANDING
REGARDING CONFIDENTIALITY

I understand that there is *no* guarantee that any information I give in interviews or answers I give on forms will be kept confidential. The forms I complete will not be shown directly to other family members by the investigator; however, any attorney or judge involved in this case may request to see the investigator's file, and any request of this nature will be honored.

I also understand that the investigator may be requested to testify at a court hearing in which case any information in the investigator's file, information obtained during the investigation, or information on forms may be revealed during testimony.

_____

Signature of Litigant or Child
(if child is old enough to sign
his or her name)

_____

(Date)

_____

Signature of Witness

_____

(Date)

LIST OF SEVEN MAJOR CRITERIA

(1) Continuity of relationships.
(2) Quantity of child care involvement.
(3) Quality of child care involvement.
(4) Flexibility regarding visitations.
(5) Non-judgmental attitude — trying to encourage child to have positive relationship with other parent.
(6) Psychological parent.
(7) Ability to individualize needs of child or children (child oriented rather than being self-centered).

FORM FOR INTERVIEWING LITIGANTS

Please number the following items (a through g), placing a (1) next to the most important item, (2) next to the second most important item, etc. until all have been rated. *Please use your own ideas and values as a guide in completing this section.*

Please sign your name and put today's date on each form completed.

There are seven (7) separate items listed.

(a) Trying to get custody of your child or children.

(b) Your child's physical and emotional health.

(c) Achieving your own goals such as employment-related goals or goals related to your social life (*goals directly related to you only*).

(d) Having time for relaxing recreational activities.

(e) Being liked by other people.

(f) Spending time with your child.

(g) Having a lot of material possessions.

FORM UTILIZED IN INTERVIEWING LITIGANTS

(Additional Questions for Litigants in Custody Cases)

(1) If you obtain legal custody of your child or children and the child wants to write and/or call the other parent, would you have any objections? Would there be any limit on frequency of calls or letters? Please give reason for your answers.

(2) If your ex-spouse refuses to pay court ordered child support payments but your child benefits from visiting your ex-spouse, would you object to the visits being continued? Please give reason for your answer.

(3) If your child wants to visit your ex-spouse at times longer than the court order specifies, would you have any objections? Please explain reason for your answer.

(4) If your ex-spouse obtains legal custody of the child or children and in the future your child does not want to visit you as often as the court order specifies, what would be your reaction?

(5) Do you have any concerns about your ex-spouse's parenting abilities? If so, what are your concerns?

(5a) Does your ex-spouse have any problems that would interfere with his ability to assume parental responsibilities for a child on a permanent basis? If answer is yes, please explain giving specific facts to substantiate.

(6) Do you and your ex-spouse disagree on any child care issues? If so, what are they and what is the nature of your disagreement?

(7) If you could only take one paid vacation day within the next month and you had a chance to participate in the activity of your choice (with or without your child or children present) what would you choose to spend the day doing and why? Would your children be with you or would they be with someone else (such as a responsible relative or babysitter)?

CHILD CARE RESPONSIBILITIES

Listed below are typical child care responsibilities experienced by parents or parent substitutes. Please be sure to place the correct number (utilizing your choices below listed 1 through 4) beside each task that applies to your situation. Please choose the answer that most closely relates to each task.

Please complete the form as it relates to your situation from the time your child or children were first born to the time you and your spouse or ex-spouse's most recent separation or divorce (or until the initiation of the current custody proceedings). Please indicate all child care tasks that not only are more recently applicable, but those that were applicable from the time of your child's birth up to the present time.

1. Usually performed by me.
2. Usually performed by my spouse or ex-spouse.
3. Usually performed by both my spouse or ex-spouse and me.
4. Usually performed by another person; if this is the most correct answer, please list name of person who usually performs the task as well as the person's relationship to the child or children after the number.

CHILD CARE TASK OR ACTIVITY

(1) Waking child up each morning.
(2) Seeing that child eats breakfast.
(3) Dressing child.
(4) Selecting child's clothes.
(5) Seeing that child goes to school.
(6) Preparing meals for child.
(7) Taking the child to doctor's appointments.
(8) Taking the child to dentist appointments.
(9) Enrolling child in school.
(10) Talking with school staff in regard to child's progress.
(11) Attend school functions such as open house.
(12) Taking care of child during child's illness.
(13) Bathes child.
(14) Changing diapers.
(15) Washing child's hair.
(16) Getting child ready for bed.
(17) Taking child for haircuts.
(18) Taking child's temperature during illness.
(19) Taking child to specialist if indicated.
(20) Potty training.
(21) Purchases clothes for child.
(22) Helps child with school work.
(23) Reading to child.
(24) Talking to child about daily events.
(25) Playing with child.
(26) Seeing that child gets to bed at a designated time.
(27) Selects gifts for child for holidays such as Christmas or birthdays.
(28) Spending time teaching values to child.
(29) Answering child's questions.
(30) Discussing with child concerns a child expresses.
(31) Supervising child.
(32) Taking child to day care and/or school program.
(33) Seeing that child practices good personal hygiene.
(34) Provides child with educational opportunities.

(35) Spends time in recreational activities with child.
(36) Disciplines child when needed.
(37) Assumes responsibility for the majority of child care tasks.

TRUE-FALSE QUESTIONS FOR LITIGANTS

Please answer the following true or false questions. Circle a T for true or an F for false after each statement based on your beliefs and values.

T F 1. My memories of my childhood are basically happy.

T F 2. When I was a child, I was disciplined at times in a manner that resulted in a bruise, mark or other injury.

T F 3. I believe that corporal punishment is the most effective method of discipline.

T F 4. If disciplining a child results in injury to the child (bruise, mark or other injury), the discipline should be considered to be abusive.

T F 5. There are times when it is frustrating to be a parent.

T F 6. If I had a chance to start all over the years before I became a parent, I would be happier if I did not become a parent.

T F 7. Some of my happiest memories are occasions I am spending with my child or children in recreational or educational activities.

T F 8. I enjoy having times that I can relax and not have parental responsibilities (even if it's for a few hours a day or a day at a time).

T F 9. My mother and/or dad used to spend time with me in recreational activities when I was growing up.

T F 10. I have had or currently have a problem with drugs and/or alcohol.

T F 11. One or more of my relatives has physically or sexually abused a child in the past.

T F 12. When a child is two years old or four years old, it is normal for a child to behave in negative ways that are usually frustrating to parents.

T F 13. If I had a choice, I would never want to spend any time away from my child or children.

T F 14. Being a parent has joys and frustrations.

T F 15. It is important for children to spend as much quality time as possible with both parents.

T F 16. If I had a choice, I would not permit my child or children to visit the other parent.

T F 17. Children's needs should be given priority over a parent's needs.

COMPLETION FORM FOR LITIGANTS

1. If my child was physically fighting with another child, I would
———————————————————————————.

2. If my child began shouting profanities directed at me, I would
———————————————————————————.

3. If my child had a temper tantrum in a grocery store, I would
———————————————————————————.

4. A child's behavior I would have difficulty dealing with would be
———————————————————————————.

5. If I discovered my child (four years old) taking a piece of bubblegum out of the store without my knowledge, I would ————————————.

6. If my child began making fun of another person, I would ————————
———————————————————————————.

7. If my child accidentally broke a neighbor's window with a baseball, I would ———————————————————————————.

8. Typical stages of child development include the:

    "————————————" twos.   "————————————" fours.
    "————————————" threes.   "————————————" fives.

9. Typical behavior of a two-year old is ————————————————————
———————————————————————————.

10. An infant needs to learn ————————————————————————————.

11. If my child had a temperature of 102 degrees, I would ————————————
———————————————————————————.

12. If a babysitter was with my child for the evening, I would be certain
———————————————————————————.

13. I would like to take my child ————————————————————————————.

14. The usual amount of time I spend with my child each day in recreational or educational activities is ————————————————————.

15. It is necessary to attend school activities ————————————————————
———————————————————————————.

16. The appropriate age to teach a child sex education is ————————————.

17. One of the most recent problem areas any parent needs to be educated about is ————————————————————————————.

COMBINATION COMPLETION TRUE–FALSE FORM
FOR LITIGANTS

1. Three of my best friends are _____.
2. In selecting friends, I try to select friends with the following qualities:
   _____.
3. My child prefers to live with _____.
4. If I had to select one factor in my spouse's or ex-spouses's lifestyle that would concern me the most, it would be _____.
5. Recording telephone conversations of my child's conversations with my spouse or ex-spouse _____.
6. If my child decided to quit school when 15½ or 16 years old, I would
   _____.
7. If my child wants to drink alcoholic beverages or use marijuana while a teenager, I would _____.

T F 1. I permit my child to have friends visit in our home.

T F 2. I have concerns about my spouse or ex-spouse's friends.

T F 3. My spouse's or ex-spouse's current lifestyle adversely affects our child.

T F 4. I would allow smoking and/or drinking alcoholic beverages in front of my child.

T F 5. I would or have permitted persons of the opposite sex as myself to stay all night in my home.

T F 6. It is better to leave some subjects such as about sex or AIDS as subjects that should not be discussed with children.

T F 7. I have or would tape record conversations of my child regarding custody issues if it would help my court case.

COMPLETION FORM FOR LITIGANTS

Please complete each sentence with the first ideas that come to your mind.

1. An example of the most educational activity or opportunity I personally provided for my child was _____.

2. One of the most nutritional meals a child could have would include _____.

3. My spouse's or ex-spouse's parental strengths include _____.

4. My spouse's or ex-spouse's parental weaknesses include _____.

5. An educational TV program beneficial for children to watch would be _____.

6. If I hear persons relating negative information or criticisms about my ex-spouse or spouse in front of my child, it would be best to _____.

7. One of the most difficult experiences related to divorce would include _____.

8. If my child wanted me to attend a program he or she would be participating in the same night I planned to attend a game or concert, I would probably _____.

9. If my child wants to choose an occupation different from what I would prefer would be chosen, it would be best to _____.

10. If I only had a week left to live, I would _____.

11. If I were physically incapable of taking care of my child or children, it would be best to _____.

12. I would like to be remembered as _____.

13. If I have plane tickets to leave for vacation and the day before I am to leave my child is hospitalized for the first time, I would _____.

14. If I won $10,000, I would _____
_____.

15. One of the worst mistakes a parent can make is to _____
_____.

16. If my son or daughter were sick, he or she would feel better if
_____.

17. The main reason my spouse or ex-spouse wants custody of our child or children is because _____
_____.

FORM FOR LITIGANTS

Please circle any opportunity or experience listed below (if any) that you would object to your son or daughter experiencing. *Keep in mind that it is assumed that each experience would be at a time that was age appropriate for your son or daughter to participate in each activity, your son or daughter is not opposed to the opportunity, and your son or daughter would not be in any danger.*

1. Opportunity to play with and get to know children of other races or cultures.
2. Opportunity to play with and get to know children of other socio-economic backgrounds.
3. Opportunity to associate with children who have physical problems (such as epilepsy or multiple sclerosis).
4. Opportunity to visit museums.
5. Learn a foreign language.
6. If attends college, being able to have a roommate who is a different race than your son or daughter.
7. Eat food from other cultures or countries.
8. Attend (as a visitor) a church service that is a different denomination than you attend or are the most familiar with.
9. An opportunity to talk to an inmate incarcerated at one of the prisons in this vicinity.
10. An opportunity to travel to other countries.
11. A chance to do volunteer work in a ghetto.
12. A chance to do work with alcoholics.
13. An opportunity to work with drug addicts.
14. An opportunity to do volunteer work in a mental hospital.
15. An opportunity to work with juvenile delinquents.
16. A chance to attend a lecture given by a person who was previously a prostitute but now tries to help teenagers *not* be involved in illegal activities.
17. An opportunity to become friends with a foreign exchange student from another country.

If you have circled any of the above opportunities indicating your objection to your son or daughter participating in the activity circled, please list your reasons for your opposition below and/or on the back of this form.

TRUE–FALSE QUESTIONS FOR LITIGANTS

Please answer the following true or false questions. Circle a T for true or an F for false after each statement based on your beliefs and values.

T F 1. If my spouse or ex-spouse did not have so many faults, our marriage would have been successful.

T F 2. If a child cannot live with both parents, it is important that they take sides and express their preference to both parents so that it is clear where the child's loyalties lie.

T F 3. If your child lives with you for several years and you have legal custody and later on your child expresses a desire to live with the non-custodial parent, the child's wish should not be given serious consideration.

T F 4. Children should appreciate the fact that if it was not for them, I would not be in this mess now.

T F 5. Children should not express their ideas or opinions on important issues concerning them.

T F 6. I find it difficult to say anything positive about my spouse or ex-spouse.

T F 7. I would be happier if my spouse or ex-spouse would be denied any visitation rights.

T F 8. I try to get detailed information about my spouse or ex-spouse from my child after each visit my child has with my spouse or ex-spouse.

T F 9. If my child refused to visit my spouse or ex-spouse, I would permit my child to not visit even if I did not know any legitimate reason for my child's refusing to visit.

T F 10. If my child is old enough to get an allowance, I would expect him or her to pay for his own telephone calls to my spouse or ex-spouse.

T F 11. I believe it would be wise for people to wait longer before having responsibilities of raising children.

T F 12. I was sexually abused when I was a child.

T F 13. I was physically abused when I was a child.

T F 14. I find it difficult to express affection to my child.

T F 15. If I lost custody in court, I would actually be relieved.

T F 16. Children have a responsibility to meet the needs of their parents.

T F 17. I am happier when my child does not enjoy being with my spouse or ex-spouse.

COMPLETION FORM FOR LITIGANTS

Please complete each sentence with the first ideas that come to your mind.

1. The happiest memory of my childhood was when I _____
_____.

2. I become the most angry when _____
_____.

3. I am sad whenever _____
_____.

4. The happiest times in being a parent include _____
_____.

5. The most frustrating part of being a parent is _____
_____.

6. The famous person I have the most respect for is _____
_____.

7. I would love to spend just one day _____
_____.

8. My greatest fault is _____.

9. My spouse's or ex-spouse's greatest fault is _____
_____.

10. It definitely is being abusive to a child if a person _____
_____.

11. A child is being neglected when _____
_____.

12. If I could have just one wish, it would be to _____
_____.

13. The most difficult part about a divorce and/or contested custody situation is _____.

14. The most frustrating age of a child to cope with is age _____ because _____.

15. I can be pleased with the job I have done as a parent if _____
_____.

16. Children can always benefit from _____.

17. Being a parent is comparable to _____.

FORM FOR LITIGANTS

Please circle any item below which either currently or in the past pertains directly to you, one of your children, your spouse or ex-spouse, a relative, or any person who is currently a member of your household.

1) Alcoholism.
2) Drug addiction.
3) Mental illness.
4) Any disease diagnosed to be terminal.
5) AIDS.
6) Has physically or sexually abused a child (determined by Department of Children and Family Services investigator).
7) Neglected a child (determined by Department of Children and Family Services investigation).

FORM FOR LITIGANTS

Please list at least seven interests, hobbies or activities your child or children enjoy the most. If more than one child, list the name of the child next to the list that pertains to that child. Also include a checkmark (V) after any activity listed that you participate in with your child.

COMPLETION FORM FOR LITIGANTS

1) I would describe my relationship with my parents as being _____ _____.

2) The main method of discipline my parents used when I was a child was _____.

3) The most traumatic event in my life that I have had to deal with so far is _____.

4) The happiest event in my life so far was _____.

5) The main qualities that attracted me to my spouse or ex-spouse were _____.

6) The main problems in my marriage were _____.

7) I would describe my spouse or ex-spouse as being _____ _____.

8) The most upset I have ever been with my child or children was _____.

9) The main disagreement I would have with my spouse or ex-spouse about child care would be _____.

10) The usual amount of time I spend directly in activities with my child each day is _____.

11) If I found out a teenage child of mine got drunk, I would _____ _____.

12) One of the most valuable lessons any person can learn is _____ _____.

13) A quality I really admire is _____.

14) My child probably would say that what he or she likes best about me is _____.

15) My child would probably say that what he or she likes least about me is _____.

16) My child would probably say that what he or she likes best about my spouse or ex-spouse is _____.

17) My child would probably say that what he or she likes least about my spouse or ex-spouse is _____.

COMPLETION FORM FOR LITIGANTS

1) The main rules or expectations I have for children are the following:
_____.

2) My spouse or ex-spouse's four best qualities are _____
_____.

3) I would like to be remembered as _____.
4) The biggest mistake I ever made was _____.
5) If my child wanted to visit my spouse or ex-spouse on a holiday not specified in the court order, I would _____
_____.

6) I would describe my child's relationship with my spouse or ex-spouse as _____.
7) The most serious trouble I have ever been in is _____
_____.

8) Three of the best gifts any person could ever receive are: _____
_____.

9) A typical day when I am with my child or children would include _____.
10) If I got paid a salary for taking care of my child, I would expect to get paid _____.
11) My best parenting skills include _____.
12) If a book were written about my life, it should be entitled _____
_____.

13) My child's preference is to live with _____.
14) When I talk about my spouse or ex-spouse in front of my child, I usually make _____ comments.
15) If my child needed to be in the hospital and only one parent could be in the room, _____ would be my child's choice.
16) If I could have one dream come true, it would be _____
_____.

17) Since court action was initiated, my child has lived with _____
_____.

COMPLETION FORM FOR CHILDREN

Please complete any questions that you can complete without any difficulty. *Please sign your name and put today's date on each form you complete.*

1) If I were stranded on an island, I would feel best if I were rescued by
_____ .

2) If I wanted to have friends stay at my house for a few days _____ would be the most accepting of my friends visiting.

3) If my dad ever got any kind of award, it would probably be for
_____ .

4) If my mom ever got any kind of award, it would probably be for
_____ .

5) My mom and dad used to have most of their arguments about
_____ .

6) The parent who spends more time in activities with me is _____
_____ .

7) The parent who seems the most negative about the other parent is
_____ .

8) The parent I have spent the most time with since I was born is
_____ .

9) The parent who would be the most likely to take me to a museum or an educational program is _____ .

10) If I wanted to visit one of my parents at a time that wasn't a scheduled visit, the parent who would be the most willing for me to visit the other parent would be _____ .

11) If I wanted to go to a movie and both my parents had other plans, _____ would be the most willing to change plans to go with me.

12) If I were the judge, I would decide that _____ would be the best parent to have permanent custody of me and/or other children.

13) The main reason my mom wants custody is _____ .

14) The main reason my dad wants custody is _____ .

15) The parent who seems to consider my ideas and feelings the most is _____ .

16) The parent who has qualities that I would most like to have myself is _____.

17) The parent I feel most relaxed with the majority of the time is

_____.

COMPLETION FORM FOR CHILDREN

Please complete all the questions below that you can complete without any difficulty.

1) My mom often says that dad _____.
2) My dad often says that mom _____.
3) The parent who helps me most with homework is _____.
4) A book written about my mom should be called _____.
5) A book written about my dad should be called _____.
6) I like to be treated like _____ treats me.
7) Dad places the most importance on _____.
8) Mom places the most importance on _____.
9) _____ has the most patience with me.
10) _____ talks to me the most about topics I am interested in.
11) I would rather spend holidays with _____.
12) _____ is more willing to take me places that I enjoy the most.
13) My dad's best quality is _____.
14) My mom's best quality is _____.
15) The parent who makes me feel the most special and worthwhile is _____.
16) The parent who says the most negative statements in general is

_____.

17) The saddest I have ever been is _____

_____.

TRUE-FALSE FORM FOR CHILDREN

Please circle the answer (T for true or F for False) that is the most correct.

T F 1) I have had a bruise, mark or other injury as a result of discipline.

T F 2) I have been touched in places that made me feel uncomfortable.

T F 3) My mom usually doesn't say anything positive about my dad.

T F 4) My dad usually doesn't say anything positive about my mom.

T F 5) My dad would be happier if I didn't want to spend time with mom.

T F 6) My mom would be happier if I didn't want to spend time with dad.

T F 7) I feel under the most pressure when I'm with my dad.

T F 8) I feel under the most pressure when I'm with my mom.

T F 9) My dad asks a lot of questions about my visits with mom.

T F 10) My mom asks a lot of questions about my visits with dad.

T F 11) My dad should be given custody by the judge.

T F 12) My mom should be given custody by the judge.

T F 13) I have thought at times that life is not worth living.

T F 14) My mom has a problem with drinking alcoholic beverages.

T F 15) My dad has a problem with drinking alcoholic beverages.

T F 16) My dad has hit me in places other than on my buttock area.

T F 17) My mom has hit me in places other than on my buttock area.

COMPLETION FORM FOR CHILDREN

Please complete each sentence with the first ideas that come to your mind.
1. The famous person my dad reminds me of is _____
    _____.
2. The famous person my mom reminds me of is _____
    _____.
3. I am happiest when _____
    _____.
4. I am saddest when _____
    _____.
5. My mom becomes the most angry when _____
    _____.
6. My dad becomes the most angry when _____
    _____.
7. If I could change one thing about my dad, it would be _____
    _____.
8. If I could change one thing about my mom, it would be _____
    _____.
9. If I were in the hospital and only one parent could stay in the room
    with me, I would choose _____ to be with me.
10. If I could go to any place I chose for a day (such as to Six Flags)
    and I could only take one of my parents, I would want to go
    with _____.
11. The parent who would be the most willing to help me if I got in
    trouble would be _____.
12. The happiest time I have had with my mom was _____
    _____.
13. The happiest time I have had with my dad was _____
    _____.
14. The famous person I like best is _____.
15. If I had $100, I would _____
    _____.
16. I am really looking forward to the day when _____
    _____.
17. When I get out of school, I would like to _____
    _____.

COMPLETION FORM FOR CHILDREN

Please complete each sentence with the first ideas that come to your mind.

1. If I won $500, I would want to _____.
2. If I feel real sad, I would feel better talking to _____
    _____.
3. My dad and I enjoy _____.
4. My mom and I enjoy _____.
5. If I got into trouble, I would want to talk to _____.
6. If I had a big secret, I would feel more comfortable discussing it
    with _____.
7. It would be easier to deal with my parent's divorce if mom would
    _____.
8. It would be easier to deal with my parent's divorce if dad would
    _____.
9. I feel under the most pressure regarding the custody issue when
    _____.
10. If I felt unhappy, I would want to be with _____.
11. What I like best about my mom is _____.
12. What I like best about my dad is _____.
13. My happiest times are _____.
14. My friends have the most fun with me when _____
    _____.
15. The most fun I have ever had was _____.
16. If I were sick, I would want to be with _____.
17. The person who makes me feel the most worthwhile and important
    is _____.

ADDITIONAL QUESTIONS TO UTILIZE IN
INTERVIEWING CHILDREN

Please respond to those questions which apply to your situation. If your answer includes more than one person, please indicate.

(1) Who prepares your meals?

(2) Who usually selects your clothes?

(3) Who enrolls you in school?

(4) Who takes you to the doctor for appointments?

(5) Who takes you to the dentist?

(6) Who attends school functions such as an open house at school?

(7) Who usually takes care of you when you are sick?

(8) Who takes you to get your hair cut?

(9) Who takes your temperature when you are sick?

(10) Who gives you medicine when it is needed?

(11) Who helps you with your homework?

(12) Who plays with you most of the time?

(13) Who takes you to day care or school?

(14) Who talks to you if you have questions or want to talk about daily activities?

(15) If you had to be in the hospital for a few days and only one person could be with you in your room, who would you choose to be with you and why?

(16) Who usually disciplines you when needed?

(17) Who supervises your daily activities (including your (17a) personal hygiene, (17b) your recreational activities, (17c) your assigned tasks around the house, (17d) school assignments, and (17e) other daily activities.

FORM LETTER TO SEND TO SCHOOL
IF SCHOOL AGE CHILDREN

Date

Re: _____

(Address)

Dear

Our agency has been ordered by the _____ County Court to complete a custody investigation in regard to _____. An important part of our investigation is obtaining a report on each child's progress in school of all school-age children involved in custody litigation.

I would appreciate it if the enclosed form could be completed by the person at school who has the most first-hand information regarding the above-named child. Please return the completed form in the enclosed self-addressed, stamped envelope at your earliest convenience.

Thank you for your cooperation in this regard.

Very truly yours,

Mary E. Lindley, MSW, CSW

MEL:ds
enclosure
Date mailed:

SCHOOL REPORT FORM TO BE UTILIZED
IN CUSTODY INVESTIGATIONS

NAME OF CHILD _____

CHILD'S BIRTHDATE _____

CHILD'S PARENTS OR PARENT SUBSTITUTE _____

CHILD'S ADDRESS _____

GRADE IN SCHOOL _____

NAME OF SCHOOL _____

ADDRESS OF SCHOOL _____

TELEPHONE NUMBER OF SCHOOL _____

Please indicate the current academic functioning of the above child.

Is child working up to his potential at the present time? If answer is no, please list reasons if known.

Please summarize child's appearance including personal hygiene. Is child currently exhibiting any behavior problems? If so, please describe the problems and include any specific relevant information.

Has child ever been absent or tardy for reasons other than reasons considered acceptable by school staff? If answer is yes, please indicate number of times during this school year child has been absent or tardy and reasons, if known.

Please summarize child's adjustment socially.

Have school staff been contacted by any family member regarding the child's progress in school? If answer is yes, please specify who has contacted school staff, frequency of contacts, and the nature of the contacts.

Do you know if any family member helps the above-named child with school work? If answer is yes, please specify name of person that helps with work and the reason you believe child receives help from person listed.

Have school staff ever initiated contacts with a relative of child that resulted in no response? If so, please explain in some detail.

Does child ever discuss his home situation? If so, please summarize any relevant information concerning child's home situation.

Does child ever express a preference regarding where he would like to live on a permanent basis? If answer is yes, please specify the child's stated preference and reasons, if known.

_____

(signature of person completing form)

_____

(title of person completing form)

_____

(date form completed)

Please attach additional sheets if needed; *also indicate if you would like to discuss this particular case with the worker in person.*
I authorize verification of the above information as part of the custody investigation.

_____   _____
(Date)   (Signature of Litigant)

_____   _____
(Date)   (Signature of Litigant)

_____   _____
(Date)   (Signature of Witness)

Date: _____

Re: _____

_____ Circuit Court

Dear

I would appreciate it if you would complete the enclosed form as soon as possible and return the completed form to our office at the above address.

I appreciate your cooperation in this regard.

Very truly yours,

Mary E. Lindley, MSW, CSW

MEL/ds
enclosure

LAW ENFORCEMENT FORM

Re: _____ Custody

Litigants: _____

DOB: _____

_____

DOB: _____

Our agency has been ordered by _____ County Court to complete a custody investigation regarding the above-named litigants. An important part of this investigation is to obtain verification of whether or not each litigant has had any involvement with the law enforcement officials in terms of charges or court convictions. Please complete this form and return the completed form in the enclosed self-addressed envelope at your earliest convenience. Please note the litigant's signed authorization at the bottom of this form acknowledging their consent for you to provide requested information.

I want to thank you in advance for your cooperation.

1. Has above named litigant ever had charges filed against him or her? _____ If answer is yes, please list specific charges, appropriate dates and the outcome of each charge (if known).

_____

_____

_____

_____

2. Have there been any court convictions regarding the above-named litigant? _____ If answer is yes, please list specific court convictions including appropriate dates.

_____

_____

_____

_____

3. Has the above-named litigant or any relative of the litigant ever been involved in any criminal behavior directly related to children? If answer is yes, please explain.

_____

_____

_____

_____

_____   _____
            Date   Signature of Person Completing Form

I authorize verification of the above information as part of the Custody Investigation.

_____   _____
            Date   Signature of Litigant

_____   _____
            Date   Signature of Witness

COLLATERAL FORM

Re: _____ Custody

Litigants: _____

_____

Our agency has been ordered by the _____ Circuit Court to complete a custody investigation regarding the above-named litigants. An important part of this investigation is to obtain relevant first-hand observations of collaterals.

Please answer the following questions that you could answer based on facts (such as your own personal observations of the above litigant's interactions with the child or children involved in the above named contested custody case).

Please return your completed form in the enclosed self-addressed envelope. The returned forms completed by collaterals are *not* submitted with my report to the court, but the information is beneficial in trying to obtain as complete a picture as possible regarding the parenting abilities of the litigants.

Please attached additional sheets of paper if necessary to relate your observations.

In answering each question please specify the name of the litigant you are relating observations about so it is clear which facts pertain to which litigant.

I want to thank you in advance for your cooperation in sharing any relevant observations or other facts you have that pertain to this particular custody case. *Be certain that you list facts to substantiate your answer to each question you respond to.*

1. Do you know only one or both litigants involved in this case? _____ M F
2. Are you related to either one of the litigants? _____ If the answer is yes, please indicate which litigant you are related to and the nature of your relationship with that person. _____
3. Have you had opportunities to observe one or both litigant's interaction with their child or children? _____. If answer is yes, please summarize your observations in regard to each litigant. _____

_____
_____
_____
_____
_____

4. Please summarize each litigant's parental strengths. _____
_____
_____
_____
_____
_____

5. Please summarize each litigant's parental weaknesses. _____
_____
_____
_____
_____

6. Do you have any knowledge of either litigant having any problem that would interfere with his or her ability to assume parental responsibilities on a permanent basis? _____ If answer is yes, please specify facts to substantiate this.
_____
_____
_____
_____

7. Do you have any facts or observations to substantiate any of the following? If answer is yes, please summarize facts relating to each question and answer that you personally are able to substantiate.

   A. Which litigant has spent the greatest amount of time in assuming responsibilities for child care tasks? _____
   _____
   _____
   _____
   _____

   B. Which litigant has spent more time in recreational activities with the child or children? _____
   _____
   _____

_____
_____
_____

C. Which litigant has provided more educational opportunities for the child or children or provides better quality care? _____

_____
_____
_____
_____

D. Which litigant is better able to focus on the needs of children?

_____
_____
_____
_____

E. Which litigant has provided the most daily care of the child or children since the litigant's separation? _____

_____
_____
_____
_____

F. Which litigant seems to be more willing to encourage a positive relationship between his spouse or ex-spouse and child? _____

_____
_____
_____
_____

G. Which litigant would provide the best role model for a child?

_____
_____
_____
_____

_____   _____
    Date   Signature of Person Completing Form

(Please do not forget to sign your name on the appropriate line above and indicate the date you completed the form.)

VERIFICATION OF EMPLOYMENT FORM

Re: _____ Custody

Litigants: _____

_____

Our agency has been ordered by the _____ County Court to complete a custody investigation regarding the above-named litigants. An important part of this investigation is to obtain verification of employment. Please complete this form as it relates to the above-named litigants and return the completed form in the enclosed self-addressed envelope at your earliest convenience.

Please note litigant's signed authorization at the bottom of this form acknowledging consent for you to provide requested information.

1. Job title of litigant, if still currently employed by you.

   _____

2. Date current employment began: _____.
3. Amount of gross monthly salary: _____.
4. Hours of employment: _____.
5. Please indicate if there are any problems regarding job performance. _____

   _____

   _____

   _____

_____   _____

Date   Signature of Person Completing Form

I authorize verification of the above information as part of the Custody Investigation.

_____   _____

Date   Signature of Litigant

_____   _____

Date   Signature of Witness

INDEX

169

ABOUT THE AUTHOR

Mary E. Lindley is currently a Department of Children and Family Services child welfare specialist in the Harrisburg, Illinois office and is currently specializing in conducting court-ordered child custody investigations in a seven county area. She also has responsibility for follow-up services for clients. This author is Supervisor of all student interns having field placement in the Harrisburg office. She has approximately seventeen years of Department of Children and Family Services experience, working in all areas including completing investigations of alleged abuse and/or neglect, providing follow-up services for clients, and working with problem teenagers. Previously the author worked two years as caseworker for the Department of Public Aid, and two years as a rehabilitation counselor at Jacksonville State Hospital, in addition to two summers of employment at the Illinois State Psychiatric Institute in Chicago. The author's educational background includes a B.A. degree (major in Sociology—Social Work Concentration), and a minor in Psychology from Southern Illinois University, as well as an M.S.W. from the University of Illinois. The author is also a certified social worker in the State of Illinois. During the completion of this worker's Master's degree her worker's field placement was in the Olney Mental Health Clinic. The author has previous experience in counseling in a mental health setting as well as being responsible for conducting group therapy sessions with patients in a psychiatric facility. The author has completed courses in rational-emotive therapy as well as in numerous in-service training sessions and workshops dealing with completing assessments.

This author completes an average of approximately seventy-seven investigations of persons within a year and, on the average, has ten to fourteen pending investigations at any given time. This author has extensive experience testifying in court during contested custody proceedings.

This author has been asked to participate in a work group whose function would be formulating Department of Children and Family Services policy revisions in regard to custody. To this author's knowledge, this author is the only child welfare specialist in the State of Illinois employed by the Department of Children and Family Services who specializes in conducting court-ordered child-custody investigations.

Currently this author is co-author with Dr. Gordon Plumb (psychologist) of a book regarding custody. This author has met eligibility requirements for listing in the National Association of Social Workers *Register of Clinical Social Workers* as well as meeting qualifications for Diplomate of Clinical Social Work. This author has also been accepted for inclusion in *Who's Who Among Human Service Professionals* for the 1988 Edition.